Readings in Literary Criticism 9
CRITICS ON D. H. LAWRENCE

Readings in Literary Criticism

CRITICS ON
D. H. LAWRENCE

Readings in Literary Criticism

Edited by W. T. Andrews

University of Miami Press
Coral Gables, Florida

CONTENTS

INTRODUCTION

This book is mainly a record of the development of Lawrence criticism in England and the Commonwealth since the time of the publication of D. H. Lawrence's first novel, *The White Peacock*, in 1911. It is accordingly hoped that students of Lawrence will find the book a useful complement to Mark Spilka's *D. H. Lawrence, A Collection of Critical Essays* (1963), in the well-known *Twentieth Century Views* series, which contains mainly extracts from the work of American critics on Lawrence since 1953. The scope of this present book is wider, revealing the full extent of the modern 'critical renaissance' of Lawrence, as Spilka puts it, which began in England as well as in many other parts of the world in the early nineteen-fifties.

Lawrence was English—'English in the teeth of all the world, even in the teeth of England', as he once wrote in a letter from Australia. F. R. Leavis has thus been right in stressing that Lawrence cannot be understood without full reference to his Englishness. The fact is everywhere apparent in his fiction and travelogues, even though he spent the greater part of his writing-life away from England, writing about places and people at times hardly known to the English imagination. Nobody but an Englishman could have written *The Plumed Serpent* or *Sea and Sardinia*, for example. Yet Lawrence's emotional and intellectual horizons were obviously far wider—and remain wider today, despite jet-travel facilities—than those of his countrymen who on the whole may still prefer to confine themselves to the 'Home Counties'. Lawrence's undoubted Englishness is counterbalanced by the equally important fact that his incurable nomadism and sheer imaginative quickness drove him to become the first truly international English novelist of indisputably major rank.

Lawrence began as a regional novelist like Hardy, but ended as a world-novelist, or as a novelist of the world, in a sense beyond the capacity of any English novelist before him or since (not excepting his great contemporary, Conrad, who was not English by birth, and who adopted England as his home when his travels were over). Despite his Englishness, Lawrence by contrast virtually rejected England, including English provincialism and post-war English decadence (in novels such as *The Lost Girl* and *Women in Love*), returning to England only for occasional brief visits. It is therefore fitting and inevitable that Lawrence criticism over the years should take roughly the same course, spreading and diverging until now it has become international in scope. For instance, much of the best critical work on Lawrence recently has come from British academics working in Australia.

A word is due to the early English critics of Lawrence during his lifetime and for a decade or so after his death. Admittedly, much of this early criticism is primarily a record of English bewilderment in the face of an undeniably English genius refusing to conform, even on the surface, to the mythically conventional pattern of English life. Without all these preliminary squabbles and confusions, however, it is to be doubted whether the present 'critical renaissance' of Lawrence could have taken place. Moreover, a point in defence of this early criticism is that a good deal of it is far from being as misguided, and as uncompromisingly hostile, as notably F. R. Leavis has been at pains to make out. On the contrary, over the space of his first three novels at least, Lawrence was met with his fair share of not entirely ignorant understanding and sympathy. It was only when confronted with the outright 'revolutionary' fiction of *The Rainbow* and *Women in Love,* together with the knowledge that Lawrence had married a German in time of war, that the English parochial conscience became seriously disturbed.

Lawrence *was* recognized, even though his faults as a novelist (his 'formlessness', for example) were increasingly urged against him at the stage when both his patriotism and his morality seemed in question. Even so, his worst enemies were forced by their recognition of his genius to be in two minds about him. Take Middleton Murry. The record shows that Murry was honestly out of his depth in his attempts to understand Lawrence: he loved and hated Lawrence, and appreciated or reviled his work, merely as his own temporary whims dictated. Hence the notorious attack upon *Women in Love,* along with its insights (Murry was the first to point to the falsity of the Birkin-as-Pharaoh passage, which Leavis himself used, years afterwards, as an illustration of Laurentian 'jargon'). Yet Murry did on occasions struggle to be fair: witness his repentant praise of Lawrence's next novel—utterly inferior and shapeless by comparison—*Aaron's Rod.* At this distance, the truth about Middleton Murry appears to be that he knew, often against his will, that Lawrence had something vital to offer, only he did not know quite what.

One of the important functions of the novelist is to perplex and disturb. It remains to be added that, for as long as Lawrence continues to puzzle and provoke his world-wide audience, interest in him will survive. As, implicit in the nature of his work, there are still plenty of problems which the modern 'critical renaissance' has failed to settle, and is unlikely to settle in the future, his reputation seems 'safe'—paradoxically much safer than that of his more orthodox literary rival, T. S. Eliot.

University of the West Indies, Barbados, 1970   W. T. ANDREWS

ACKNOWLEDGEMENTS

We wish to thank the following for permission to reprint copyright material from the works listed below.

British Printing Corporation (review in *The Bookman*); *The Critical Review*, University of Melbourne, and the authors (G. B. McK. Henry's *Carrying On: 'Lady Chatterley's Lover'* and T. B. Tomlinson's *Lawrence and Modern Life: 'Sons and Lovers', 'Women in Love'*); Curtis Brown Ltd and the author (W. H. Auden's *Some Notes on D. H. Lawrence*); *Essays in Criticism* (Roger Dataller's *Elements of D. H. Lawrence's Prose Style* and F. H. Langman's *'Women in Love'*); Faber and Faber Ltd and Northwestern University Press (H. M. Daleski's *The Forked Flame: A Study of D. H. Lawrence*); Faber and Faber Ltd and the Viking Press Inc. (*Letters of James Joyce*, edited by Stuart Gilbert); The Hogarth Press, Quentin Bell, Angelica Garnett and Harcourt Brace Jovanovich, Inc. (Virginia Woolf's Notes on D. H. Lawrence in *Collected Essays*, I; from *The Moment and Other Essays* by Virginia Woolf, copyright, 1948, by Harcourt Brace Jovanovich, Inc. and reprinted with their permission); Max Kester Ltd (Introduction to Aldous Huxley's *The Letters of D. H. Lawrence*); *Meanjin Quarterly* (Curtis Atkinson's *Was There Fact in D. H. Lawrence's 'Kangaroo'?*); Modern Language Association of America (Edward Engelberg's *Escape from the Circles of Experience*); Mouton and Co., The Hague (George A. Panichas's *Adventure in Consciousness: The Meaning of D. H. Lawrence's Religious Quest*); *The New Statesman* (reviews in *The Athenaeum*, *The Nation and Athenaeum* and *The New Statesman and Nation*); Laurence Pollinger Ltd, the Estate of the late Mrs Frieda Lawrence, William Heinemann Ltd and the Viking Press Inc. (D. H. Lawrence's *'Autobiographical Sketch'* in *Phoenix II*); Martin Secker and Warburg Ltd (Catherine Carswell's *The Savage Pilgrimage*); *The Spectator* (reviews by Richard Church, V. Sackville-West and Lord David Cecil); University of Chicago Press and the author (Eugene Goodheart's *The Utopian Vision of D. H. Lawrence*). We have been unable to trace the copyright owners of two reviews from *The Saturday Review*, and would welcome any information which might enable us to do so.

Critics on D. H. Lawrence: 1911-1930

DAVID HERBERT LAWRENCE (1885-1930)

It was while I was at Croydon, when I was twenty-three, that the girl [Jessie Chambers] who had been the chief friend of my youth, and who was herself a school teacher in a mining village at home, copied out some of my poems, and without telling me, sent them to the *English Review*, which had just had a glorious rebirth under Ford Madox Hueffer.

Hueffer was most kind. He printed the poems, and asked me to come and see him. The girl had launched me, so easily, on my literary career, like a princess cutting a thread, launching a ship.

I had been tussling away for four years, getting out *The White Peacock* in inchoate bits, from the underground of my consciousness. I must have written most of it five or six times, but only in intervals, never as a task or a divine labour, or in the groans of parturition.

I would dash at it, do a bit, show it to the girl; she always admired it; then realize afterwards it wasn't what I wanted, and have another dash. But at Croydon I had worked at it fairly steadily, in the evenings after school.

Anyway, it was done, after four or five years' spasmodic effort. Hueffer asked at once to see the manuscript. He read it immediately, with the greatest cheery sort of kindness and bluff. And in his queer voice, when we were in an omnibus in London, he shouted in my ear: 'It's got every fault that the English novel can have.'

Just then the English novel was supposed to have so many faults, in comparison with the French, that it was hardly allowed to exist at all. 'But,' shouted Hueffer in the bus, 'you've got GENIUS.'

This made me want to laugh, it sounded so comical. In the early days they were always telling me I had got genius, as if to console me for not having their own uncomparable advantages.

From 'Autobiographical Sketch', in *Assorted Articles, 1928–1929*. (London, Martin Secker, 1930).

ANONYMOUS

(D. H. LAWRENCE AS A WOMAN NOVELIST)

This novel is a characteristic specimen of the modern fiction which is being written by the feminine hand. The older ideas and ideals are sacrificed ruthlessly to an attempt to breathe vitality into a succession of cinematographic pictures illustrative of the lives of the *dramatis personae*. There is, however, no selection, as this method would suggest; impressions are merely scattered at random. It is, as it were, paulo-post-Impressionism in fiction. That there is cleverness in this modern study of nerves is obvious from the first chapter, but it is equally impossible to avoid the conclusion that the characters were spun in the author's brain. There is no verisimilitude. Farmer's daughters talk high culture, and an ordinary reader's head whirls in trying to determine the social relations of the sundry people involved. Scenes seem introduced merely because the author has observed them or thought of them, not because they add anything to the plot, or even to the atmosphere. Such is the modern method which a growing school of writers in this country encourages, but which, as we have pointed out before, owes its conception rather to Zola than to English sources.

The author of *The White Peacock* is never realistic with the crudity of the master, but she is needlessly frank to a fastidious mind. As the trend of the novel in general seems to be in this direction, she should be successful, particularly when she has learnt her craft better. There are suggestions, and even more than suggestions, of the making of a fine style in her writing.

Review of *The White Peacock* in *The Athenaeum*, February 10, 1911.

ANONYMOUS

The merely average writer, with half a dozen mediocre novels to his credit, can show that he has learnt to make his thoughts flow in a carefully regulated stream from one given point to another. The result may, or may not, be a tolerable imitation of nature, but it will probably be called a readable book if the writer has learnt certain tricks of his craft. Men make canals, and nature can only make rivers, and canals are infinitely more convenient for navigation. It must be confessed that Mr Lawrence's thoughts flow after the manner of a river, rapid from its source which is in the mountains, taking its course to the sea with windings which must be a scandal to the trained engineer. Most novels, on the other hand, are on the canal pattern; chapter headings stand at regular intervals like poplars planted along the bank, and each tells us that we have got so much nearer to the desired end. Mr Lawrence has shown no such consideration for the reader who always likes to know exactly where he is, but has left his tale and its characters to explain themselves. Incident and dialogue are recorded as in a diary which is for no stranger's eye. The book contains characters and events which do not seem to aid the progress of the plot, but, even when certain rough and seemingly hurried notes on the lives of a few men and women annoy from their seeming lacking of reason, force and power are never absent. A mirror has been held up to nature, and more has been reflected in it than could be conveniently crowded into a conventional novel. In *The White Peacock* the rough tone of the remoter country places has been caught, and, in his bucolic passages, the author seems almost to rival the skill of Mr Thomas Hardy. The chapter which tells how they cut the corn in a Derbyshire harvest-field and how they drove out and hunted the rabbits is worth many volumes of an ordinary man's correct writing. Dominating the whole story is the magnificent creature, George, aspiring from the soil he rules to the stars which he can never reach. His rise from a happy animalism to the possession of a soul, and his final fall to the lowest depths of conscious degradation, form the central ideas of the tale, but there are lesser characters who can interest us almost as much. Lettie and Emily are splendidly contrasted types of women: the one constant and submissive, the other wayward and proud; the one praying for love, the other exacting it as her due. The whole book is a wonderful portrait gallery, and not the worst of its figures is that of the teller of the story, the man who saw everything that concerned others and eventually forgot himself.

The Saturday Review, May 13, 1911.

ANONYMOUS

(SONS AND LOVERS—'A NOVEL OF QUALITY')

There is occasionally a fitness in the association of a particular publisher with a particular book and that of Messrs Duckworth & Co. with *Sons and Lovers*, Mr D. H. Lawrence's latest novel, is an example of it. The book has naturally a place in a list which includes such authors as John Galsworthy, Cunninghame Graham and Charles Doughty, to name only three of the many who have enriched the literature of today with work which is, in some sense, esoteric . . . It has nothing of urbanity and no trace of the humorous and faintly contemptuous patronage which is common—and probably rather difficult to avoid—in novels dealing with a particular piece of country and class of people. Its descriptions and interpretations are convincing as experience is convincing; Mr Lawrence is on his own ground and presents it with an assured intimacy of knowledge that never fails or blurs. It is Derbyshire and Nottingham of which he writes, the Derbyshire in which the grime of coal-mines is close neighbour to open country of singular charm, and the quality of it is in the very texture of his story.

The sons and lovers of the title-page are the sons of Gertrude Morel, who married a miner and lived in the Bottoms of Bestwood. Mr Lawrence wastes sympathy on none of his characters; it is much if he gives them an approving word; but Mrs Morel is drawn at fullest length, as faithfully as if he loved her. Her husband, a fine and florid animal at the time of her marriage, is shallow and futile, a creature of easy appetites easily slaked; the book comes upon her at a time when she has to suffice for herself in all that side of her life which is responsible and not merely material. She was clear headed, faithful to her ideas of right, full of strength and purpose, and with it she did not lack her spice of shrewishness.

It was with her children that she was successful, and chiefly so with her second son, Paul, the most notable and by far the most complex and ineffectual lover of them all. He shares with his mother the centre of Mr Lawrence's stage; for him her harsh righteousness tones itself to a softer key. With his diffidence and fastidiousness there goes a strain of the artist; he has the makings of a painter in him; he concludes by being extraordinarily ineffectual both as a lover and a man; but it is the author's gift to show him as not the less real for that. It is impossible to summarize the tale of his emotional adventures; there is hardly anything in the book that can be conveyed at all in synopsis, the whole of it develops itself so truly that there is scarcely an episode which would not lose significance if it were detached from its context.

It is a novel of outstanding quality, singular in many respects and in none more so than in the author's constancy to his artistic purpose, which never suffers him to see his people in a dramatic or spectacular light or on a level higher or lower than his own. The fact that they exist suffices him without calling them names, whether good or bad, his business is to show them, dispassionately and accurately. He writes with a nervous pliancy which is a joy to read.

The Bookman, August 1913. Signed P.G.

FORD MADOX HUEFFER (1873-1939)

The book is a rotten work of genius. It has no construction or form—it is execrably bad art, being all variations on a theme. Also it is erotic.

Reported remark on *The Trespasser.* See Richard Aldington, *Portrait of a Genius, but . . . ,* 1950, p. 96.

EZRA POUND (1885-   )

Lawrence, as you know, gives me no particular pleasure . . . Hueffer, as you know, thinks highly of him. I *recognize* certain qualities of his work. If I were an editor I should probably accept his work without reading it. As a prose writer I grant him first place among the younger men.

Letter to Harriet Monroe, London, September 23, 1913.

ANONYMOUS

This book reveals a strong and vivid imagination; a faculty of seeing and describing the country-side that can spring only from a true love of nature combined with poetic insight; and no inconsiderable power of dealing impressively, if not always convincingly, with psychological problems.

The Rainbow, like Mr Lawrence's earlier novel, *Sons and Lovers*, is a family piece, but of a far more ambitious character. The first chapter introduces us to the Brangwens, yeomen farmers who had lived for generations on the borderland of Derbyshire and Nottinghamshire, and sets the stage for the piece with the marriage of Tom Brangwen to Lydia Lensky, the widow of a Polish political incendiary and refugee, and the daughter of a Polish noble by a German wife. Lydia has a four-year-old little girl, Anna. The story is one of three generations, being concerned with the successsive loves of Tom Brangwen and Lydia Lensky, of their nephew Will Brangwen and Anna Lensky, and of Ursula Brangwen, daughter of the latter couple, and Anton Skrebewsky, a son of another Polish exile by an English wife.

In the story we find no attempt to deal with the possibilities latent in the mating of an aristocratic Polish stock with Midland yeomen. The intermixture appears to be nothing more than the introduction of an unknown factor in order to mask the improbabilities introduced, and the result is an increasing discord between the principal actors and the setting. The minor characters are human beings, and fit better into the scheme.

We must say a word or two concerning the freedom Mr Lawrence has allowed himself in his treatment of sexual matters. It is often difficult to decide whether such realism is justified or not, but much that is to be found here is, in our opinion, undeniably unhealthy.

The Athenaeum, No. 4594, November 13, 1915.

G. W. DE TUNZELMANN

The suppression of *The Rainbow* last Saturday has brought into prominence its doctrines and their exposition by Mr Lawrence. I was one of those who had occasion to read the book before the reviews appeared. It was not pleasant to read, and its unpleasantness increased steadily from start to finish. Yet I read it through with an interest that likewise increased as I read, in spite of this unpleasantness and in spite of the artistic defects indicated in your review.

B

As a work of art, and therefore as a novel, it is, in my humble opinion, a hopeless failure. To me the interest of the book consists in the fact that each one of the principal characters is a sincere, and in many ways a powerful, development of a psychological hypothesis underlying much of Mr Lawrence's recent work. If he had only recognized the fact of his artistic failure and traced it to its source, the utter falsity of his hypothesis, of which *The Rainbow* is an unconscious *reductio ad absurdum,* he might well have recast the latter into a work of art. For then he might have written with due restraint, and presented us with an object lesson at least as valuable as that of the drunken helots to the youth of Sparta. Unfortunately, however, he has become so enamoured of his hypothesis that he has allowed himself to treat its most repulsive consequences with what evidently the court considered loving appreciation. This has led him into what many, I fear, may regard as salaciousness, tending to stimulate the perfectly legitimate sexual impulses and appetites into morbid excesses, in defiance of the universal experience that they stand in need not so much of stimulation as of regulation and control by the will.

The sense of isolation of the individual spirit must at some time or another have oppressed every thinking man and woman. The author assumes this spiritual isolation to be absolute, and susceptible only of more or less imperfect and transient masking by a sort of conscious absorption in the material environment. This masking is assumed to find its most complete expression in sexual intercourse, which is, therefore, to be glorified in itself, and freed from every semblance of restraint.

This is but one of the many futile attempts to reconcile the facts of existence with the materialistic pseudophilosophy which has proved such a powerful instrument for the debasement of the German nation. And many of the humiliating weaknesses which have so hampered our action against Germany may be traced to the too great readiness which has been shown in accepting this same pseudophilosophy at the hands of those whom we are at last united in recognizing as our foes—in things spiritual as well as in things temporal.

Editor's Note:
We print this letter from a contributor who had discussed with us the questions he now raises before the courts had given their decision as to Mr Lawrence's novel, and had asked our permission to write to us.

Letter to *The Athenaeum,* No. 4595, November 20, 1915.

ANONYMOUS
('THE DECAY OF MR D. H. LAWRENCE')

There are two ways in which we may approach Mr Lawrence's new novel: we may regard it either as one among the many, or as marking a phase in the development of one who was by far the most promising, and is still among the most interesting, of the writers of the younger generation. From the former angle it is an interesting book, and there is little more to be said.

But when we consider it as a novel by Mr D. H. Lawrence, it becomes a different thing, which interests us differently. The very fact that it is a well-constructed, competently written tale of a girl who breaks away from the sterility of middle-class life in a mining district to form a passionate marriage with an Italian, has another importance; for if we compare *The Lost Girl* with *Sons and Lovers,* we remark that the increase of control of a kind is set off by a very obvious loss of imaginative power. Mr Lawrence is now, as a novelist, commensurable with his contemporaries. *The Lost Girl* is certainly a better novel than most of his coevals could write, but it is largely of the same kind as their novels. *Sons and Lovers* was not; neither was *The Rainbow.* In them there were flashes of psychological intuition, passages of darkly beautiful writing, so remarkable that at times they aroused a sense that the latest flowering on the tree of English literature might be one of the most mysterious.

There is not very much mystery about *The Lost Girl.* Alvina Houghton springs from the same country as Paul Morel; but it is no longer the country of a miraculous birth. Woodhouse is as real, and real in the same way, as Mr Bennett's *Five Towns;* there is no garment of magical beauty flung over it, like that which gleamed out of the opening pages of *Sons and Lovers.* And in Alvina herself we catch sight of none of the strange potencies that seemed to hover about Paul Morel. We are interested in her; she is perfectly credible; she is even mysterious: but the mystery in her is not that of a revelation of the unknown, but rather of an ignorance in her creator. She is more the idea of a woman than a woman. It is as though Mr Lawrence had lost some power of immediate contact with human beings that he once possessed; his intuitive knowledge has weakened under the pressure of theory. But whereas the beauties of *The Rainbow* could be held in the mind very separate from the sex-theory which dominated and falsified the book, the texture of *The Lost Girl* is much more closely knit. We can no longer separate the true from the false; the theory impinges on the imaginative reality at every point. We lose our grasp of the central characters just at the moment when it should be firmest. A phrase like 'his dark receptivity overwhelmed her' will intrude at a crisis in the love between Alvina and her Italian lover, Cicio; and the effect is as though the writer's (and therefore the reader's) consciousness had suddenly collapsed. The woman and the man are lost in the dark. What we are told of them may be true; or it may be false: we cannot tell with our waking minds. Mr Lawrence becomes most esoteric when he should be most precise, for nothing is more esoteric than the language of a theory peculiar to oneself—and, we might add, nothing is uglier.

We are not merely bewildered but repelled when Mr Lawrence writes in this way of the effect of an actor's imitation of another man upon his heroine:

> Louis was masterful—he mastered her psyche. She laughed till her head lay helpless on the chair, she could not move. Helpless, inert she lay, in her orgasm of laughter. The end of Mr May. Yet she was hurt.

And it is always through language as vague as this, if less positively ugly, that we are made to grope for the reality of the emotional crises of Mr Lawrence's story.

Mr Lawrence's own grasp of the central theme of his story, of the peculiar attraction which held Alvina and Cicio together, despite an amount of ecstatic hatred that would have sufficed to separate a hundred ordinary lovers for ever, may possibly be profound; but he does not convey it to us. He writes of his characters as though they were animals circling round each other; and on this sub-human plane no human destinies can be decided. Alvina and Cicio become for us like grotesque beasts in an aquarium, shut off from our apprehension by the misted glass of an esoteric language, a quack terminology. Life, as Mr Lawrence shows it to us, is not worth living; it is mysteriously degraded by a corrupt mysticism. Mr Lawrence would have us back to the slime from which we rose. His crises are all retrogressions.

In short, we are nonplussed by Mr Lawrence's fifth novel. For a little while we inclined to explain the obvious loss of creative vigour as a paralysis produced by the suppression of *The Rainbow*; but the cause proved to be inadequate. Mr Lawrence's decline is in himself. Even in the final chapters which describe how Alvina accompanies Cicio to his home in the Italian mountains, we miss some essential magic from the passion of his descriptive writing. We cannot suppose that it was fear of the censor that stayed his hand here.

The Athenaeum, December 17, 1920. Signed M.

J. MIDDLETON MURRY (1889-1957)

(THE NOSTALGIA OF MR D. H. LAWRENCE)

Mr Lawrence is set apart from the novelists who are his contemporaries by the vehemence of his passion. In the time before the war we should have distinguished him by other qualities—a sensitive and impassioned apprehension of natural beauty, for example, or an understanding of the strange blood bonds that unite human beings, or an exquisite discrimination in the use of language, based on a power of natural vision. All these things Mr Lawrence once had, in the time when he thrilled us with the expectation of genius: now they are dissolved in the acid of a burning and vehement passion. . . .

Women in Love is five hundred pages of passionate vehemence, wave after wave of turgid, exasperated writing impelled towards some distant and invisible end; the persistent underground beating of some dark and inaccessible sea in an underworld whose inhabitants are known by this alone, that they writhe continually, like the damned, in a frenzy of sexual awareness of one another. Their creator believes that he can distinguish the writhing of one from the writhing of another; he spends pages and pages in describing the contortions of the first, the second, the third, and the fourth. To him they are utterly and profoundly different; to us they are all the same. And yet Mr Lawrence has invented a language, as we are forced to believe he has discovered a perception for them. The eyes of these creatures are 'absolved'; their bodies (or their souls: there is no difference in this world) are 'suspended'; they are 'polarized'; they 'lapse out'; they have, all of them, 'inchoate' eyes. In this language their unending contortions are described; they struggle and writhe in these terms; they emerge from dark hatred into darker beatitudes; they grope in their own slime to some final consummation, in which they are utterly 'negated' or utterly 'fulfilled'. We remain utterly indifferent to their destinies, we are weary to death of them.

At the end we know one thing and one thing alone: that Mr Lawrence believes, with all his heart and soul, that he is revealing to us the profound and naked reality of life, that it is a matter of life and death to him that he should persuade us that it is a matter of life and death to ourselves to know that these things are so. These writhings are the only real, and these convulsive raptures, these oozy beatitudes the only end in human life. He would, if he could, put us all on the rack to make us confess his protozoic god; he is deliberately, incessantly, and passionately obscene in the exact sense of the word. He will uncover our nakedness. It is of no avail for us to declare and protest that the things he finds are not there; a fanatical shriek arises from his pages that they are there, but we deny them.

If they are there, then indeed it is all-important that we should not deny them. Whether we ought to expose them is another matter. The fact that European civilization has up to the advent of Mr Lawrence ignored them can prove nothing, though it may indicate many things. It may indicate that they do not exist at all; or it may indicate that they do exist, but that it is bound up with the very nature of civilization that they should not be exposed. Mr Lawrence vehemently believes the latter. It is the real basis of his fury against the consciousness of European civilization which he lately expounded in these pages in a paper on Whitman. He claims that his characters attain whatever they do attain by their power of going back and re-living the vital process of pre-European civilization. His hero, Rupert

Birkin, after reaching the beginning of 'consummation' with his heroine, Ursula Brangwen, is thus presented:—

> He sat still like an Egyptian Pharaoh, driving the car. He felt as if he were seated in immemorial potency, like the great carven statues of real Egypt, as real and as fulfilled with subtle strength, as these are, with a vague, inscrutable smile on the lips. He knew what it was to have the strange and magical current of force in his back and loins, and down his legs, force so perfect that it stayed him immobile and left his face subtly, mindlessly smiling. He knew what it was to be awakened and potent in that other basic mind, the deepest physical mind. And from this source he had a pure and magic control, magical, mystical, a force in darkness, like electricity.

Through such strange avatars his characters pass, 'awakened and potent in their deepest physical mind'. European civilization has ignored them. Was it from interested motives, or do they indeed exist?

Is Mr Lawrence a fanatic or a prophet? That he is an artist no longer is certain, as certain as it is that he has no desire to be one; for whatever may be this 'deep physical mind' that expresses its satisfaction in 'a subtle, mindless smile,' whether it have a real existence or not, it is perfectly clear that it does not admit of individuality as we understand it. No doubt Mr Lawrence intends to bring us to a new conception of individuality also; but in the interim we must use the conceptions and the senses that we have. Having these only, having, like Sam Weller in the Divorce Court, 'only a hordinary pair of eyes', we can discern no individuality whatever in the denizens of Mr Lawrence's world. We should have thought that we should be able to distinguish between male and female, at least. But no! Remove the names, remove the sedulous catalogues of unnecessary clothing—a new element and a significant one, this, in our author's work—and man and woman are indistinguishable as octopods in an aquarium tank.

The essential crisis of the book occurs in a chapter called, mystically enough, 'Excurse'. In that chapter Rupert and Ursula, who are said to reach salvation at the end of the history, have a critical and indescribable experience. It is not a matter of sexual intercourse, though that is, of course, incidentally thrown in; but it has a very great deal to do with 'loins'. They are loins of a curious kind, and they belong to Rupert. Mr Lawrence calls them 'his suave loins of darkness'. These Ursula comes 'to know'. It is, fortunately or unfortunately, impossible to quote these crucial pages. We cannot attempt to paraphrase them; for to us they are completely and utterly unintelligible if we assume (as we must assume if we have regard to the vehemence of Mr Lawrence's passion) that they are not the crudest sexuality. Rupert and Ursula achieve their esoteric beatitude in a tea-room; they discover by means of 'the suave loins of darkness' the mysteries of 'the deepest physical mind'. They die, and live again. After this experience (which we must call x):

> They were glad, and they could forget perfectly. They laughed and went to the meal provided. There was a venison pasty, of all things, a large broad-faced cut ham, eggs and cresses and red beetroot, and medlars and apple-tart and tea.

We could not resist quoting the final paragraph, if only as evidence that 'the deepest physical mind' has no sense of humour. Why, in the name of darkness, 'a venison pasty, *of all things*'? Is a venison pasty more incongruous with this beatitude than a large ham? Does the 'deepest physical mind' take pleasure in a tart when it is filled with apples and none when it is filled with meat?

We have given, in spite of our repulsion and our weariness, our undivided attention to Mr Lawrence's book for the space of three days; we have striven with all our power to understand what he means by the experience x; we have compared it with the experience y, which takes place between the other pair of lovers, Gudrun and Gerald; we can see no difference between them, and we are precluded from inviting our readers to pronounce. We are sure that not more than one person in a thousand would decide that they were anything but the crudest kind of sexuality, wrapped up in what Mr S. K. Ratcliffe has aptly called the language of Higher Thought. We feel that the solitary person might be right; but even he, we are convinced, would be quite unable to distinguish between experience x and experience y. Yet x leads one pair to undreamed-of happiness, and y conducts the other to attempted murder and suicide.

This x and this y are separate, if they are separate, on a plane of consciousness other than ours. To our consciousness they are indistinguishable; either they belong to the nothingness of unconscious sexuality, or they are utterly meaningless. For Mr Lawrence they are the supreme realities, positive and negative, of a plane of consciousness the white race has yet to reach. Rupert Birkin has a negroid, as well as an Egyptian, avatar; he sees one of those masterpieces of negro sculpture to which we have lately become accustomed. It is not 'the plastic idea' which he admires:

> There is a long way we can travel after the death-break; after that point when the soul in intense suffering breaks, breaks away from its organic hold like a leaf that falls. We fall from the connection with life and hope, we lapse from pure integral being, from creation and liberty, and we fall into the long African process of purely sensual understanding, knowledge in the mystery of dissolution. He realized now that this is a long process—thousands of years it takes, after the death of the creative spirit. He realized that there were great mysteries to be unsealed, sensual, mindless, dreadful

mysteries, far beyond the phallic cult. How far, in their inverted culture, had these West Africans gone beyond phallic knowledge? Very, very far. Birkin recalled again the female figure: the elongated, long, long body . . . the long imprisoned neck, the face with tiny features like a beetle's. This was far beyond the phallic knowledge, sensual, subtle realities far beyond the scope of phallic investigation.

We believe Mr Lawrence's book is an attempt to take us through the process. Unless we pass through this we shall never see the light. If the experiences which he presents to us as part of this process mean nothing, the book means nothing; if they mean something, the book means something; and the value of the book is precisely the value of these experiences. Whatever they are, they are of ultimate fundamental importance to Mr Lawrence. He has sacrificed everything to achieve them; he has murdered his gifts for an acceptable offering to them. Those gifts were great; they were valuable to the civilization which he believes he has transcended. It may be that we are benighted in the old world, and that he belongs to the new; it may be that he is, like his Rupert, 'a son of God'; we certainly are the sons of men, and we must be loyal to the light we have. By that light Mr Lawrence's consummation is a degradation, his passing beyond a passing beneath, his triumph a catastrophe. It may be superhuman, we do not know; by the knowledge that we have we can only pronounce it subhuman and bestial, a thing that our forefathers had rejected when they began to rise from the slime.

The Nation and The Athenaeum, August 13, 1921.

*   *   *

A year ago, reviewing Mr Lawrence's last novel, which seemed to us full of noxious exasperation, we said that he was an elemental force, perhaps the only one in modern English literature. With him criticism was unavailing and irrelevant; we must 'let determined things to destiny Hold unbewailed their way'.

Well, they have held their way for another year, with a result that we could not have prophesied. Mr Lawrence's sun shines forth after the darkness of eclipse. The exasperation, the storm and stress are gone. He has dragged us with him through the valley of the shadow; now we sail with him in the sunlight. Mr Lawrence's new book ripples with the consciousness of victory; he is gay, he is careless, he is persuasive. To read *Aaron's Rod* is to drink of a fountain of life.

Mr Lawrence is like the little girl. When he is good, he is very, very good; and when he is bad, he is horrid. Now we feel that he will never be horrid again, but go on from strength to strength, until the predestined day when he puts before the world a masterpiece. For Mr Lawrence is now, indisputably, a great creative force in English literature.

We have always believed he was that potentially; even when we have crusaded against him, we have merely been paying tribute to his power. No other living writer could drive us to a frenzy of hostility as he has done; no other fill us with such delight.

Aaron's Rod is the most important thing that has happened to English literature since the war. To my mind it is much more important than *Ulysses*. Not that it is more important in and for itself than Mr Joyce's book. No doubt it is a smaller thing. But *Ulysses* is sterile; *Aaron's Rod* is full of the sap of life. The whole of Mr Joyce is in *Ulysses*; *Aaron's Rod* is but a fruit on the tree of Mr Lawrence's creativeness. It marks a phase, the safe passing of the most critical phase in Mr Lawrence's development. He has survived his own exasperation against the war. We did not doubt that if he did survive it, he would survive it splendidly; but after *Women in Love* we doubted deeply whether he would survive at all. *Women in Love* seemed to show him far sunk in the maelstrom of his sexual obsession.

Aaron's Rod shows that he has gained the one thing he lacked: serenity. Those who do not know his work may read it and wonder where the serenity is to be found. They must read all Mr Lawrence's work to discover it fully. They must allow themselves to be manhandled and shattered by *The Rainbow* and by *Women in Love* before they can appreciate all the significance of his latest book. For the calm is but partly on the surface of *Aaron's Rod,* it lies chiefly in the depths. As before, Mr Lawrence offers a violent challenge to conventional morality; as before, he covers us with the spume of his ungoverned eloquence. But the serenity is there. Mr Lawrence can now laugh at himself without surrendering a jot of his belief in the truth he proclaims. It is as though he looked back whimsically at his own struggling figure in the past, saw all his violence and extravagance, and recognized that he could not have become what he is if he had not been what he was.

Not that *Aaron's Rod* is a perfect book; it is very far from that. It is, indeed, in some ways an extremely careless book. A lady who is Josephine Hay on one page becomes Josephine Ford—for no reason —in the next. At another moment the author clean forgets that Lilly, who is, with Aaron Sisson, the chief character in the book, has not been through the war. Then it has a positive carelessness, also, which is purely refreshing. Mr Lawrence breaks off a couple of pages of splendid psychological presentation with this:

> Don't grumble at me then, gentle reader, and swear to me that this damned fellow wasn't half clever enough to think all these smart things, and realize all these fine-drawn-out subtleties. You are quite right, he wasn't, yet it all resolved itself in him as I say, and it is for you to prove that it didn't.

It takes a big man to be able to do that nowadays without breaking the spell. Mr Lawrence's spell is not broken: he is a big man. He exults in his strength. He is so exultant that he really doesn't trouble to carry on his book—after page 200. When he has brought us to the point at which we are completely absorbed in the relation between Aaron and Lilly, he fobs us off with a passionate adventure of Aaron's, important enough in its way, but of which we know the conclusion beforehand, and three or four pages of conversation between them.

We could riddle the book with criticism, but not one of the shafts would touch its soul. It is real; it is alive. We have seen it said of *Aaron's Rod* by a well-known critic that whereas the presentation of the characters is vivid, the author's philosophizing is (as usual) esoteric and portentous. That is not true. Mr Lawrence's philosophizing in this book is as vivid and vital as the rest. He is tackling a real problem and offering a real solution, and we think the philosophizing is, if anything, even better than the characters. Perhaps that is because we happen to agree with it. But to talk of Mr Lawrence's philosophizing at all is misleading; he is not and never has been a philosopher; he is and always has been a moralist. Sometimes we have thought him a pernicious one. In the light of *Aaron's Rod,* we see him as a man who has experimented deeply and sincerely with human relationship in the determination to find some bedrock on which to build. Sometimes, in the torment of his search, he has wrapped up his experiences in the jargon of a mystical metaphysic. Now, having found what he sought, with the solid simplicity of conviction beneath his feet, he speaks plainly and persuasively.

That, we think, is the word for *Aaron's Rod*. With all its imperfections, all its carelessness, all the host of minor characters who refuse to become properly substantial—we judge them by Mr Lawrence's own standards of achievement—it is persuasive. The style rings with the same clear truth as the message. Mr Lawrence offers happiness; he points a way to security, and his words have the carelessness of confidence. No longer, as has been the case with his books of late, have we to content ourselves with sudden brief visions of shining beauty in the midst of inspissated and writhing darkness, like the shimmering rush of the bride out of the wedding carriage at the beginning of *Women in Love*. There is beauty everywhere in *Aaron's Rod*, beauty of the thing seen, beauty of the seeing spirit; and everywhere the careless riches of true creative power. *Aaron's Rod*—truly symbolic name—satisfies Arnold's test of magic of style. It is life-imparting.

After all that, it is most irrelevant to mention what the book 'is about'. It is simply the story of the effort of a man to lose the whole world and gain his own soul. Aaron Sisson leaves his wife, though he loves her and knows that he loves her, because he feels instinctively that she is engulfing him. He never returns to her in the book; neither does he ever deny the reality of the bond between them. Aaron is the instinct to which Lilly supplies the consciousness; and we are left with an indication that between these two men there is eventually to be a profound and lasting friendship. Mr Lawrence's theme is the self-sufficiency of the human soul. The book convinces us that he at least is within a measurable distance of having attained it.

The Nation and the Athenaeum, August 12, 1922.

*   *   *

... I have never felt so passionately angry against any book as I did against *Women in Love*. I know why. Lawrence was deliberately plunging into the abyss, down, down into the depths, far, far away from the light of the intellectual consciousness. I hate abysses. But I also know that big men do have to plunge into them if they are to bring up something new. Really new, not a clever, empty rearrangement of the old parrot-ideas, without passion or potency.

In *Fantasia of the Unconscious* Lawrence produces a new and living thing. He sets himself to answer the old question: 'Sir, what must I *do* to be saved? And, for my own part, I believe his to be a true answer. There is a great deal about plexuses and ganglia and nodes and polarization. Whether that is, in fact, true, I do not know, and it would not matter in the least if a physiologist came forward to demonstrate that it was all balderdash, just as an astronomer will doubtless prove that his notion that it is we who keep the sun going is nonsense. I know what Lawrence means by it all, and I believe that what he means is true. And, anyhow, it's a gorgeous book to read. It is a draught of pure life, bubbling from the living rock. It is the work of a *man*. 'It is the most important work', say the publishers, 'which has appeared since Nietzsche's *Zarathustra*.' They are nearer to the truth than most publishers manage to be. Amended to 'the most important book of the *Zarathustra* kind since *Zarathustra*', it is true.

The Nation and The Athenaeum, March 31, 1923.

J. D. BERESFORD (1873-1947)

D. H. Lawrence's *Kangaroo* stands quite apart from any of these... other novels [under review]. We may say, and quite truly, that it is hurriedly written, that it is not a story, that there is no attempt at construction in it, that except for 'Kangaroo' himself—drawn with a violence and accuracy that remind one of the old Will Dyson cartoons —the characters are of no great importance. But, having said that, we have to acknowledge without any qualification whatever that this is the work of genius, a thing separate in kind. What matters supremely to Lawrence is the search for reality among the souls of people—and of things. He may turn aside for half-a-dozen pages to describe—as no other living writer could—the colour, appearance, and life of South-East Australia; but even then it is some essence that he is searching for, and not to portray the effects of a three-dimensional world. And in

Kangaroo he has, more frankly than in his other novels, resorted to autobiography. It is not only that he has incidentally told a long, true story of his experiences in Cornwall in the course of the war; but, also, that the central character is just himself, the lonely, passionate, eager Lawrence, desperately searching for the soul of humanity, in Australia:

> ... he had nothing to do with much that is in the world of man. When he was truly himself he had a quiet stillness in his soul, an inward trust. Faith undefined and indefinable. Then he was at peace with himself. Not content, but peace like a river, something flowing and full.

Other writers may relate their stories to the deep historical past. Lawrence relates his to eternity.

The Nation and The Athenaeum, December 8, 1923.

E. B. C. JONES

With Mr Lawrence, the case is one of genius; here laziness, the accumulation of inexact expressions rather than the discovery of the precise, inevitable words, are the faults of a giant. It is a platitude by now that Mr Lawrence's philosophy is like a 'crate of smashed breakfast eggs'; but he remains, *qua* novelist, a giant; his imagination is of the highest order. He can be, to an appalling degree, merely silly, as when he writes with unction:

> It ['father complex'] is just a word invented. Here was a man who had kept alive the old red flame of fatherhood ... a great natural power.

All words are 'just words invented'; and the old red flame of fatherhood, like the old red flame of international hatred, is only too easy to keep alive; but in 'England my England', unlike its recent predecessors, the silliness is confined to this one passage, and irritation with it is lost in admiration of the superb description of Egbert's death. Here, and in 'The Primrose Path', Mr Lawrence is at his best. To have read these pages is to have experienced something with an actuality, an intensity, a stimulation of one's faculties which is the appanage of real art. When at his top pitch of creative excitement, and therefore beyond fumbling and philosophizing, Mr Lawrence is a writer of the first rank.

The Nation and The Athenaeum, February 23, 1924.

CONRAD AIKEN

Mr Lawrence's book on American literature is perhaps even more singular than one now expects a book by Mr Lawrence to be; and it is probably without exception the most singular book ever written on

American literature ... In *Studies in Classic American Literature*—as in his latest book of verse, *Birds, Beasts, and Flowers,* and (to a lesser extent) in his psychological debauch *Fantasia of the Unconscious*—he behaves like a man possessed, a man who has been assured by someone (perhaps an Analyst) that restraint is nonsense, that nothing is of importance save a violent, unthinking outpouring of feelings and perceptions; unselected, unarranged, and expressed with a conscious disregard for personal dignity. Perhaps it is Whitman's barbaric yawp which has so disturbed him. Let us, he says in effect, get rid of these literary niceties and conventions and manners, let us be naked and unashamed.

> If only people would meet in their very selves, without wanting to put some idea over one another, or some ideal.... Damn all ideas and all ideals. Damn all the false stress, and the pins.... I am I. Here am I. Where are you? ... Ah, there you are! Now, damn the consequences, we have met.

These sentences occur in Mr Lawrence's study of Cooper. Of Franklin he remarks: 'O Benjamin! O Binjum! You do NOT suck me in any longer.' Of Hawthorne: 'Old-fashioned Nathaniel, with his little-boy charm, he'll tell you what's what. But he'll cover it with smarm.' He confides in the same essay:

> I always remember meeting the eyes of a gipsy woman, for one moment, in a crowd, in England. She knew, and I knew. What did we know? I was not able to make out. But we knew.

He confides further: ' "I can read him like a book," said my first lover of me. The book is in several volumes, dear.' Discussing the flogging episode in *Two Years Before the Mast,* he writes:

> The poles of will are the great ganglia of the voluntary nerve system, located beside the spinal column, in the back. From the poles of will in the backbone of the captain, to the ganglia of will in the back of the sloucher Sam, runs a frazzled, jagged current, a staggering circuit of vital electricity....

Of Whitman:

> I AM HE THAT ACHES WITH AMOROUS LOVE. What do you make of that? I AM HE THAT ACHES. First generalization. First uncomfortable universalization. WITH AMOROUS LOVE! O, God! Better a bellyache. A bellyache is at least specific. But the ACHE OF AMOROUS LOVE! Think of having that under your skin. All that! I AM HE THAT ACHES WITH AMOROUS LOVE. Walter, leave off.... CHUFF! CHUFF! CHUFF! CHU-CHU-CHU-CHU-CHUFF! Reminds one of a steam engine.

These excerpts, while not perhaps the most striking that could be found, will serve to suggest Mr Lawrence's manner. He is nothing if

not colloquial, racy, and confidential. No trifle is too irrelevant for introduction. In his passion for the direct, for the naked and unashamed, he
insists on drawing our attention to the very odd clothes he wears
(stylistically speaking), and, not satisfied with this, flings them off
in a kind of dance of the seven veils. At bottom, this is nothing but
intellectual vanity. Mr Lawrence is convinced that anything he says,
no matter how he says it (and he tries perversely to make his saying
of it as aggressively and *consciously* and peculiarly naked as possible),
will be important. This is a great pity; for here and there, in the course
of this amazing farrago of quackeries, occultisms, ganglia, and devil-
women, Mr Lawrence observes his American subjects and their
American scene with quite extraordinary acuteness. His tracing of
the wish-fulfilment motive in the novels of Cooper and Hawthorne
would be wholly admirable if it were not so overshadowed by his
alternate efforts to be funny (which are lamentable) and to be shocking
(which are pathetic). Again, one is extremely interested in his thesis
that all art, but particularly and most persistently American art,
springs from or accompanies the attempt of man to adjust himself
to a supersensual morality. In this, he approaches (and is almost alone
in approaching) an understanding of the fact that it is the functional
nature of art which should pose for the critic his chief problem. Mr
Lawrence is consistently aware of this problem in every study here
presented; he invites us to watch with him the drama of the struggle
between man's unregenerate 'unconscious' and civilization, as it works
itself out in the 'dream' of art. Unhappily, his awareness of the problem
never leads him to define it with any care or precision. His recklessness
with terms is astounding. Logic, in his hands, achieves monsters—
fantastic structures grow, ascend, throng the universe, and disappear
into the intense inane, in the twinkling of an eye. Unhappily again,
for all the fact that he moves towards a scientific basis for criticism
and delights in the exposure of shams and shibboleths, he brings with
him as many shams and shibboleths as he destroys. He is as full of
nostrums as a Californian. His book swarms with gods (of the 'soul'),
greater and lesser; he attaches a tremendous importance to something
he calls the 'Holy Ghost'; and to complicate the situation, he is all the
time ferociously aware of the 'blood' and the 'ganglia'.

These paraphernalia, undefined and numerous, confuse Mr
Lawrence's book and make apparent, of course, his own confusion. One
comes away with a feeling that Mr Lawrence could perceive psychological and aesthetic causes with remarkable shrewdness, but that for
the most part he is prevented from a clear view by a frenzy of excitement. Life, art, and criticism of art—all, for Mr Lawrence, have in
them something feverish and sensational. He must talk about them in
terms of gods, ghosts, and nether darknesses, His own effects, in other
words (which are of a highly peculiar and tyrannous nature), are too
immediately and uncontrolledly engaged—he loses his distance. The

result, when he turns to criticism, is a kind of sensationalism—
awkward, harshly jocose, violent, and often offensive—but here and
there lighted with an extraordinarily fine bit of perception, beauti-
fully given.

The Nation and The Athenaeum, July 12, 1924.

EDWIN MUIR

The Plumed Serpent is surely the most garrulous book Mr Lawrence
has ever written. His chief vault as an executant, indeed, has always
been garrulity. He perpetually turns back, repeats himself, feels,
perhaps, that he has not said something quite as he wished to say it,
and hammers on until finally it is either not said at last, or said
magnificently. This we have come to accept, with resignation, as his
customary technique; but in the present book his wastefulness of
attack is still greater, for apparently he has never decided what to do.
He wishes to convey an impression of Mexico, he wishes to write a
story about Kate and her relations with two men, he wishes finally to
provide the age with a myth and a gospel. But he rarely succeeds in
combining the three. His descriptions of Mexico are travel impressions; his account of Kate is fiction of the same kind as *Women in Love*
and *Aaron's Rod*; and when he describes the ritual and creates the
hymns of the resurrected god Quetzalcoatl, he is a theorist, a visionary, living in a world which contains neither Kate nor Mexico. In all
three genres, and especially in the last, he occasionally excels. Some
of the earlier hymns to Quetzalcoatl are profound and beautiful. But
even in these he finally slips into that 'vain repetition' which, there
is the best authority for believing, is acceptable to God as little as to
the readers of a book. All this raises the question whether Mr Lawrence
is indeed so sincere as he seems to be. The closest parallel in modern
literature to his hymns to Quetzalcoatl is *Also Sprach Zarathustra*; but
would we have believed that Nietzsche was in earnest about his gospel
if he had incorporated it in a novel and accompanied it with a guide to
the Riviera? Mr Lawrence is an original personality, perhaps a great
writer, and his message to the age must needs, therefore, be important
and should be able to stand by itself. But that he should muffle it up in
a modern novel makes us feel that he doubts its validity; and that he
should accompany it with political animadversions on contemporary
Mexico and bursts of exasperation at white races and Indians makes
us think that it is only of ordinary importance to him. The moments
of inspiration in *The Plumed Serpent* seem to have hardly more
significance for him than the moments of futile indignation. And
even his denunciations are slip-shod; they weary us finally because
very rarely do they grip upon the definite evil. Mr Lawrence curses
largely, but he curses carelessly; and if a curse is to be of power it

must be exact. He describes the feelings which the evil of the world arouses in him; we recognize that these feelings are vivid; but the evil itself is obscured behind the emotional storm it awakens. In some of the earlier hymns to Quetzalcoatl there is greater profundity, perhaps, than Mr Lawrence has ever shown before. The new religion is made credible by the sheer loftiness of inspiration. But not even the new religion is sustained; it falls away as fatally as the book itself. Still a 'Thus Spake Quetzalcoatl,' a collection of some of the hymns in this volume, with perhaps a few more, might have been magnificent. But as it stands the book is an outpouring of anything and everything; it does not so much lose, as defeat, its effect.

The Nation and the Athenaeum, February 20, 1926.

BARRINGTON GATES

The police have hastened to review Mr Lawrence's latest poems, and in consequence, as he contemptuously admits in his preface, a dozen of them have not been printed. Whatever the political or ethical aspects of this action, it is almost certainly idiotic as a practical piece of literary criticism. For if the obscenity of Mr Lawrence exists, it exists in all his poems. You cannot profitably say 'Here he goes too far' because the lengths to which he goes are consistently equal; and it is as sensible to capture a flying atom or two exploded from this fount of furious energy as to lop off a dozen leaves of a tree because its overpowering vulgar habit offends you. The remarkable thing about Mr Lawrence is that one who lives at such a pitch of primitive feeling should be so ferociously articulate. Men who live as close to nature as he do not usually say anything at all. They express themselves in gusts of physical energy, they exult and suffer in violent silence. But with Mr Lawrence it is words that are always at the boil. The prevailing mood of his poetry is one of anger, rebellion, and contempt. He hates the mess men are now making of their lives by intellectualizing their emotions and organizing themselves into slavery. To mate, to work, to know one's desire and to fulfil it—this is to live; but to poke at sex with the mind, to work only to get money, to be cultured instead of in a glowing state of nature—this is putrefaction. The respectable man is Mr Lawrence's enemy. Accosting him everywhere, he says, 'You bloody fool, take that,' and that is delivered not with a fist but with a pen. A large proportion of the free verse explosions in this book can only claim to be poetry because they are extremely direct and telling outbursts of concentrated fury. Sometimes the claim vanishes altogether:

The only reason for living is being fully alive;
and you can't be fully alive if you are crushed by secret fear
and bullied with the threat: Get money, or eat dirt!—

and forced to do a thousand mean things meaner than your nature,
and forced to clutch on to possessions in the hope they'll make you feel
  safe,
and forced to watch everyone that comes near you, lest they've come
  to do you down—

and so on, in crude prose, as long as the human race occupies him.
But when Mr Lawrence looks at the good life of an elephant, a snake,
or a flower his fury falls away. Here is vital energy unimpeded by the
upstart mind. Mr Lawrence understands that, and celebrates it in verse
which is ennobled by an extraordinarily powerful intuitive perception:

> O flowers they fade because they are moving swiftly; a little torrent of
> life leaps up to the summit of the stem, gleams, turns over round the
> bend of the parabola of curved flight, sinks, and is gone, like a comet
> curving into the invisible.

The Mr Lawrence who has written some of the best animal poems
in the language is not different from the squirter of Billingsgate. It
is the same man, gravely at ease among his friends.

The Nation and The Athenaeum, July 27, 1929.

RICHARD CHURCH

Mr Lawrence, the human volcano, is still in eruption, still pouring the
lava of his philosophy of atavism down the slopes of his towering
personality, and annihilating the cities erected by human convention,
fear, and indolence. The singleness and powerful directness of his
genius invite this image of the volcano, but we must use it with care.
There are other qualities in him, appearing only after his fierce
struggle against the poverty, puritanism, and drabness of his early
lower-middle-class environment. He is free of that struggle now, and
though the memory lingers like malaria in his blood, making him
tremble at times with a sort of febrile anger, his more general attitude
is one of tolerance. But it is the tolerance of the tiger basking in the
sun. The complacent, the rich, the stupid, the hypocritical, need to
beware: which means, since all of us are one or other of these kinds,
that all of us need to watch that deceptive calmness.
  The essence of his faith is this:

> The blood knows in darkness, and forever dark,
> in touch, by intuition, instinctively.
> The blood also knows religiously,
> and of this, the mind is incapable.
> The mind is non-religious.

The knowledge from such a source is quick, penetrating. It gives a
sort of occult wisdom whose subtlety transcends logic and the slow

c

machinery of justice . . . But his weaknesses also spring from this source. It leads to disproportionate obsessions, and temporary blindness to the third man's point of view. As for his technique, it is unmatched. No artist has carried free-verse so far. He has the sweep and grandeur of Whitman, but with an added grace, a susceptibility to the touch of single words, vowels and consonants. The pulse of thought and emotion fills the cadence of his unmeasured line: a lovely art, so seemingly simple, so really deliberate. Here is a perfect example:

> It is a wonder foam is so beautiful.
> A wave bursts in anger on a rock, broken up
> in wild white sibilant spray
> and falls back, drawing in its breath with rage,
> with frustration how beautiful!

The Spectator, August 3, 1929.

Critics on D. H. Lawrence: 1930-1950

CATHERINE CARSWELL (1879-1946)

... His books are easy to read but hard to understand. Therein lies part of their potency. 'A book,' said Lawrence, who had pondered deeply upon such matters, 'lives as long as it is unfathomed.' Or again, 'The mind understands; and there's an end of it.' Therein also lies their vital difference from the books of such writers as Joyce or Proust, which are hard at first to read, but comparatively easy to understand once the initial difficulty is overcome. These have evolved a new technique, but they belong themselves to an outworn way of life. What they do—and it is much—is to interpret and express the old in a fresh language. Lawrence, on the contrary, except that the drum-tap and emphasis of his style are as original to himself as they are at first irritating to many readers, has elected to speak in a familiar language. But his story-shapes, his incidents, his objects and his characters are chosen primarily as symbols in his endeavour to proffer a new way of life. That there can indeed be a new way of life—though possibly only by a recovery of values so remote in our past that they are fecund from long forgetting, and as far out of mind as they are near to our blind fingers—is the single admission he seeks from his readers, as it was the belief that governed his actions. Most, however, even of those who have vocally admired him, will make any admission except just this. It includes, they know, the admission that his prescience was unique in his generation. Here is much for one man to ask of his fellows. So they prefer to continue with simplifications that are away from the point, with 'patterns' and with set phrases, which serve at the best to show how evocative Lawrence is—as a mere name more evocative than Lenin or than Freud. If Lawrence invariably committed himself, his critics infallibly give themselves away. Of all moralists he is the most demoralizing.

Introductory Note to *The Savage Pilgrimage: A Narrative of D. H. Lawrence*, London, 1932 (Revised Edition).

V. SACKVILLE-WEST (1892-1962)

Finally, in the last month, Messrs G. Orion have published a posthumous novel by D. H. Lawrence, *The Virgin and the Gipsy*. For Lawrence—the later Lawrence—this is a quiet book, screaming at nobody. It is full of the extraordinary, sensuous beauty which nobody but Lawrence could quite encompass. The gipsy in his green jersey, the encampment in the quarry, the floods coming down, the old grandmother drowned, the policeman in the ruined room in the morning, whence the naked gypsy had fled—all these things dwell in the mind with the uneasy suggestion of an undefined symbolism. One is never quite sure of what Lawrence meant; one doubts whether Lawrence himself was quite clearly sure; one is certain only that behind Lawrence's huge muddles and mistakes lay a most desperate conviction. This is no place to speak fully of Lawrence—Lawrence who shared the intensity of Tolstoy, the indignation of Carlyle, and the exuberance of Walt Whitman. It is the place only to call attention to his last book, which 'lacks the author's final revision, and has been printed from the manuscript exactly as it stands'.

The Spectator, June 28, 1930.

JAMES JOYCE (1882-1941)

... I understand from Miss Monnier that there is a big conspiracy on at the *Nouvelle Revue Française* to make a boost of Lawrence's book *Lady Chatterbox's Lover*, which is to be brought out in a form exactly similar to Lazy Molly's ditto-ditto accompanied by a campaign of articles in papers and reviews, the publication to be in French. This scheme is what Bloom would call Utopian and I cannot understand how they can expect any sensible person to pay hundreds of francs for such a production when the genuine article much more effectively done can be had in any back shop in Paris for one tenth of the money.

Letter to Harriet Shaw Weaver, September 27, 1930.

[Miss Monnier] told me that the N.R.F. angered at her refusal to give them U had decided to favour Lawrence's *Lady Chatterli's* [*sic*] *Lover* which is coming out in French. I also received a letter from a man in England who has nearly completed a long study and exegesis of this work and has obtained opinions about it from G.B.S., A.H., O.S., M.M. and E.T.C. and wants an opinion from me. These are all to be printed in front of this study and exegesis of this work. In the middle of my own work I have got to listen to this. I read the first two pages of the usual sloppy English which is a piece of propaganda in favour of something which, outside of D.H.L.'s country at any rate, makes all the propaganda for itself.

Letter to Harriet Shaw Weaver, December 17, 1931.[1] (For the full text of the above letters, see *Letters of James Joyce,* ed. Stuart Gilbert, London, 1957).

VIRGINIA WOOLF (1882-1941)

The partiality, the inevitable imperfection of contemporary criticism can best be guarded against, perhaps, by making in the first place a full confession of one's disabilities, so far as it is possible to distinguish them. Thus by way of preface to the following remarks upon D. H. Lawrence, the present writer has to state that until April 1931 he was known to her almost solely by reputation and scarcely at all by experience. His reputation, which was that of a prophet, the exponent of some mystical theory of sex, the devotee of cryptic terms, the inventor of a new terminology which made free use of such words as solar plexus and the like, was not attractive; to follow submissively in his tracks seemed an unthinkable aberration; and as chance would have it, the few pieces of his writing that issued from behind this dark cloud of reputation seemed unable to rouse any sharp curiosity or to dispel the lurid phantom. There was, to begin with, *Trespassers,* a hot, scented, overwrought piece of work, as it seemed; then *A Prussian Officer,* of which no clear impression remained except of starting muscles and forced obscenity; then *The Lost Girl,* a compact and sea-man-like piece of work, stuffed with careful observation rather in the Bennett manner; then one or two sketches of Italian travel of great beauty, but fragmentary and broken off; and then two little books of poems, *Nettles* and *Pansies,* which read like the sayings that small boys scribble upon stiles to make housemaids jump and titter.

Meanwhile, the chants of the worshippers at the shrine of Lawrence became more rapt; their incense thicker and their gyrations more mazy and more mystic. His death last year gave them still greater liberty and still greater impetus; his death, too, irritated the respectable; and it was the irritation roused by the devout and the shocked, and the ceremonies of the devout and the scandal of the shocked, that drove one at last to read *Sons and Lovers* in order to see whether, as so often happens, the master is not altogether different from the travesty presented by his disciples.

[1] In *James Joyce* (1959), Richard Ellmann records in a footnote to Chapter XXXIV, p. 628, a different version of this letter. Ellmann states: 'On December 17, 1931, he [Joyce] wrote Miss Weaver of *Lady Chatterbox's Lover*: "I read the first 2 pages of the usual sloppy English, and S.G. read me a lyrical bit about nudism in the wood and the end which is a piece of propaganda in favour of something which, outside of D.H.L.'s country at any rate, makes all the propaganda for itself." ' Ellmann records in the same footnote: 'Lawrence had reciprocal feelings about *Ulysses*; as he said to Frieda Lawrence, "The last part of it is the dirtiest, most indecent, obscene thing ever written. Yes it is, Frieda.... It is filthy." '

This then was the angle of approach, and it will be seen that it is an angle that shuts off many views and distorts others. But read from this angle, *Sons and Lovers* emerged with astonishing vividness, like an island from off which the mist has suddenly lifted. Here it lay, clean cut, decisive, masterly, hard as rock, shaped, proportioned by a man who, whatever else he might be—prophet or villain—was undoubtedly the son of a miner who had been born and bred in Nottingham. But this hardness, this clarity, this admirable economy and sharpness of the stroke are not rare qualities in an age of highly efficient novelists. The lucidity, the ease, the power of the writer to indicate with one stroke and then to refrain indicated a mind of great power and penetration. But these impressions, after they had built up the lives of the Morels, their kitchens, food, sinks, manner of speech, were succeeded by another far rarer, and of far greater interest. For after we have exclaimed that this coloured and stereoscopic representation of life is so like that surely it must be alive—like the bird that pecked the cherry in the picture—one feels, from some indescribable brilliance, sombreness, significance, that the room is put into order. Some hand has been at work before we entered. Casual and natural as the arrangement seems, as if we had opened the door and come in by chance, some hand, some eye of astonishing penetration and force, has swiftly arranged the whole scene, so that we feel that it is more exciting, more moving, in some ways fuller of life than one had thought real life could be, as if a painter had brought out the leaf or the tulip or the jar by pulling a green curtain behind it. But what is the green curtain that Lawrence has pulled so as to accentuate the colours? One never catches Lawrence—this is one of his most remarkable qualities— 'arranging'. Words, scenes flow as fast and direct as if he merely traced them with a free rapid hand on sheet after sheet. Not a sentence seems thought about twice: not a word added for its effect on the architecture of the phrase. There is no arrangement that makes us say: 'Look at this. This scene, this dialogue has the meaning of the book hidden in it.'

One of the curious qualities of *Sons and Lovers* is that one feels an unrest, a little quiver and shimmer in his page, as if it were composed of separate gleaming objects, by no means content to stand still and be looked at. There is a scene of course; a character; yes, and people related to each other by a net of sensations; but these are not there— as in Proust—for themselves. They do not admit of prolonged exploration, of rapture in them for the sake of rapture, as one may sit in front of the famous hawthorn hedge in *Swann's Way* and look at it. No, there is always something further on, another goal. The impatience, the need for getting on beyond the object before us, seem to contract, to shrivel up, to curtail scenes to their barest, to flash character simply and starkly in front of us. We must not look for more than a second; we must hurry on. But to what?

Probably to some scene which has very little to do with character, with story, with any of the usual resting places, eminences, and consummations of the usual novel. The only thing that we are given to rest upon, to expand upon, to feel to the limits of our powers is some rapture of physical being. Such for instance is the scene when Paul and Miriam swing in the barn. Their bodies become incandescent, glowing, significant, as in other books a passage of emotion burns in that way. For the writer it seems the scene is possessed of a transcendental significance. Not in talk nor in story nor in death nor in love, but here as the body of the boy swings in the barn.

But, perhaps, because such a state cannot satisfy for long, perhaps because Lawrence lacks the final power which makes things entire in themselves, the effect of the book is that stability is never reached. The world of *Sons and Lovers* is perpetually in process of cohesion and dissolution. The magnet that tries to draw together the different particles of which the beautiful and vigorous world of Nottingham is made is the incandescent body, this beauty glowing in the flesh, this intense and burning light. Hence whatever we are shown seems to have a moment of its own. Nothing rests secure to be looked at. All is being sucked away by some dissatisfaction, some superior beauty, or desire, or possibility. The book therefore excites, irritates, moves, changes, seems full of stir and unrest and desire for something withheld, like the body of the hero. The whole world—it is a proof of the writer's remarkable strength—is broken and tossed by the magnet of the young man who cannot bring the separate parts into a unity which will satisfy him.

This allows, partly at least, of a simple explanation. Paul Morel, like Lawrence himself, is the son of a miner. He is dissatisfied with his conditions. One of his first actions on selling a picture is to buy an evening suit. He is not a member, like Proust, of a settled and satisfied society. He is anxious to leave his own class and to enter another. He believes that the middle class possess what he does not possess. His natural honesty is too great to be satisfied with his mother's argument that the common people are better than the middle class because they possess more life. The middle class, Lawrence feels, possess ideas; or something else that he wishes himself to have. This is one cause of his unrest. And it is of profound importance. For the fact that he, like Paul, was a miner's son, and that he disliked his conditions, gave him a different approach to writing from those who have a settled station and enjoy circumstances which allow them to forget what those circumstances are.

Lawrence received a violent impetus from his birth. It set his gaze at an angle from which it took some of its most marked characteristics. He never looked back at the past, or at things as if they were curiosities of human psychology, nor was he interested in literature as literature. Everything has a use, a meaning, is not an end in itself. Comparing him again with Proust, one feels that he echoes nobody, continues no tradition, is unaware of the past, of the present save as it affects the future. As a writer, this lack of tradition affects him immensely. The thought plumps directly into his mind; up spurt the sentences as round, as hard, as direct as water thrown out in all directions by the impact of a stone. One feels that not a single word has been chosen for its beauty, or for its effect upon the architect of the sentence.

Notes on D. H. Lawrence, 1931, first published in *Collected Essays,* I, ed. Leonard Woolf, 1947.

LORD DAVID CECIL (1902-   )

... They [Lawrence's Letters] possess in a supreme degree the especial merits of good letters, directness, intimacy, unself-consciousness, vitality, and in certain respects they are an even more startling witness to Mr Lawrence's genius than his novels. He was above all things an intense and dominant personality. And this was not altogether an advantage to him as a novelist. A novel is first of all a picture of its characters: and Mr Lawrence's strong individuality prevented him entering into other characters. His characters are expressions of varying aspects of himself. They may look different, but, with a few rare exceptions, such as the mother in *Sons and Lovers,* they all talk the same. And all are very unlike anyone else except Mr Lawrence. In his letters he is always talking himself, he has no character to draw but himself...

And here we come to the second conspicuous fact about Mr Lawrence's letters. They are not only remarkable as literature; they are also irresistibly fascinating as a revelation of personality. But as such their effect on the reader is more ambiguous. His letters leave us sure that Mr Lawrence was a great writer, they leave us less sure that he was a great man. In some ways he was. His character lacked many faults; and signally some of those faults which characterize the literary temperament as we have learnt to know it to-day. He was not precious, or self-conscious, or feeble, or worldly. Indeed, there was something heroic about him: at moments he looms before us lit by the selfless, unearthly light of an inspired prophetic vision. And yet, and yet— when we are preparing to yield him our whole-hearted admiration, something intervenes which makes us hold it back. It is not just that he had faults, that he was always arrogant and often narrow. So was Carlyle; and Carlyle, whether we like him or not, was certainly a great man. But Mr Lawrence's character, as exposed by this correspondence, had some aspects which were not great at all. He was suspicious, he could not bear a breath of criticism. Search as we may through the long array of his letters, we never find a word of unreserved praise for anyone living or dead. It was perhaps the complement of his intense individuality that, to a greater degree than any other writer of equal eminence in England, he was an egotist. He preached contact with others as the supreme good in life. But himself he was incapable of it. For contact comes from forgetting oneself and caring for others; and this Mr Lawrence could do no more than he could swim the Atlantic. He shrank from the general herd of mankind, he could hardly bring himself to submit to their gaze in a medical examination. And his relations with his friends, so hopefully entered upon, so hotly pursued, seemed nine times out of ten to follow the same disastrous course. They were uncertain from the first; before long a word of criticism or even of disagreement would suggest to him that they were deceiving him; that, for some obscure reason, because they were rich or because they were poor, because they were old or because they were young, they were his secret and active enemies. And at once his outraged egotism rose against them in a scream of anguish. He lost all control; he screamed, he spat, he pelted mud. For, and this is his least attractive attribute, Mr Lawrence was not dignified in his wrath; when in the frenzy of his passion he tore his prophet's robes from him he stood revealed a gutter-snipe.

These defects grew on him with age. The 1929 letters lack, almost wholly, the glowing fancy and delicious playfulness which enchant us in those of 1914–15. Yet this loss does not lead us to condemn Mr Lawrence the more; indeed, it witnesses to a fact about him which should, maybe, prevent us from condemning him at all. From his earliest years Mr Lawrence was shadowed by disease. This disease, acting on his highly-strung temperament, made him an egotist, and an uncontrolled egotist. As he grew older he grew more ill, and proportionately the more egotistic and uncontrolled. But his healthy self was a good self. The real Lawrence was the fresh, flame-like, aspiring Lawrence that we admire.

The Spectator, November 18, 1932.

ALDOUS HUXLEY (1894-1963)

It is impossible to write about Lawrence except as an artist. He was an artist first of all, and the fact of his being an artist explains a life which seems, if you forget it, inexplicably strange. In *Son of Woman*, Mr Middleton Murry has written at great length about Lawrence— but about a Lawrence whom you would never suspect, from reading that curious essay in destructive hagiography, of being an artist. For Mr Murry almost completely ignores the fact that his subject—his victim, I had almost said—was one whom 'the fates had stigmatized "writer" '. His book is *Hamlet* without the Prince of Denmark—for all its metaphysical subtleties and its Freudian ingenuities, very largely irrelevant. . . .

... Explanations of him [Lawrence] in terms of a Freudian hypothesis of nurture may be interesting, but they do not explain. That Lawrence was profoundly affected by his love for his mother and by her excessive love for him, is obvious to anyone who has read *Sons and Lovers*. None the less it is, to me at any rate, almost equally obvious that even if his mother had died when he was a child, Lawrence would still have been, essentially and fundamentally, Lawrence. Lawrence's biography does not account for Lawrence's achievement. On the contrary, his achievements, or rather the gift that made the achievement possible, accounts for a great deal of his biography. He lived as he lived, because he was, intrinsically and from birth, what he was. If we would write intelligibly of Lawrence, we must answer, with all their implications, two questions: first, what sort of gifts did he have? and secondly, how did the possession of these gifts affect the way he responded to experience?

Lawrence's special and characteristic gift was an extraordinary sensitiveness to what Wordsworth called 'unknown modes of being'. He was always intensely aware of the mystery of the world, and the mystery was always for him a *numen*, divine. Lawrence could never forget, as most of us almost continuously forget, the dark presence of the otherness that lies beyond the boundaries of man's conscious mind. This special sensibility was accompanied by a prodigious power of rendering the immediately experienced otherness in terms of literary art.

Such was Lawrence's peculiar gift. His possession of it accounts for many things. It accounts, to begin with, for his attitude towards sex. His particular experiences as a son and as a lover may have intensified his preoccupation with the subject; but they certainly did not make it. Whatever his experiences, Lawrence *must* have been preoccupied with sex; his gift made it inevitable. For Lawrence, the significance of the sexual experience was this: that, in it, the immediate, non-mental knowledge of divine otherness is brought, so to speak, to a focus—a focus of darkness. Parodying Matthew Arnold's famous formula, we may say that sex is something not ourselves that makes for—not righteousness, for the essence of religion is not righteousness; there is a spiritual world, as Kierkegaard insists, beyond the ethical—rather, that makes for life, for divineness, for union with the mystery. Paradoxically, this something not ourselves is yet a something lodged within us; this quintessence of otherness is yet the quintessence of our proper being. 'And God the Father, the Inscrutable, the Unknowable, we know in the flesh, in Woman. She is the door for our in-going and our out-coming. In her we go back to the Father; but like the witnesses of the transfiguration, blind and unconscious.' Yes, blind and unconscious; otherwise it is a revelation, not of divine otherness, but of very human evil. 'The embrace of love, which should bring darkness and oblivion, would with these lovers (the hero and heroine of

one of Poe's tales) be a daytime thing, bringing more heightened consciousness, visions, spectrum-visions, prismatic. The evil thing that
daytime love-making is, and all sex-palaver!' How Lawrence hated
Eleonora and Ligeia and Roderick Usher . . . ! What a horror, too, he
had of all Don Juans, all knowing sensualists and conscious libertines!
(About the time he was writing *Lady Chatterley's Lover* he read the
memoirs of Casanova, and was profoundly shocked.) . . . To *use* love
in this way, consciously and deliberately, seemed to Lawrence wrong,
almost a blasphemy. . . .

Introduction to *The Letters of D. H. Lawrence,* 1932, pp. x-xiii.

THEODORE SPENCER (1902-1949)

(IS LAWRENCE NEGLECTED?)

The publication of this rich if uneven volume [*Phoenix*] of
Lawrence's ungathered or unpublished papers—sketches, book reviews,
essays on sex, painting, education, psychology—once more brings up
the question of Lawrence's place in recent literature. He has, in the
six years since his death, in spite of all the books about him—perhaps
because of them—been neglected. Almost nothing in the technique of
his novels has been fruitful to practising novelists, and his particular
kind of philosophy has been ignored by the central trends of our
decade.

Lawrence hated people to say that he wasn't an artist; he took
offence when Edwin Muir observed that he had not submitted himself to any discipline. But Muir was right; artistic discipline, no
matter what Lawrence may say about it, did not really absorb him.
It was what he saw, what he felt, that mattered. And what Lawrence
saw and felt was of extraordinary interest. I doubt if there has ever
been a writer who has been so remarkably aware of the immediate
present, the pulse and glow of the life-giving present, as he; nor has
there often been a writer who could convey that awareness so well.
'Give me!' he cries in the preface to *New Poems,* 'give me nothing
fixed, set, static. . . . Give me the still white seething, the incandescence
and the coldness of the incarnate moment: the moment, the quick of
all change and haste and opposition: the moment, the immediate
present, the Now.' Put in that form, of course, it sounds rather like
rant; Lawrence is not always at his best when he tries to justify or explain his intuitions. Where he is at his best is in the actual descriptions,
descriptions of a rabbit or a bird or a fox terrier (the little story in this
volume of a fox terrier named 'Rex' is Lawrence at his finest). The
same is true of Lawrence's descriptions of places—Sardinia or
Australia or New Mexico. On this level, the descriptive level,
Lawrence is a great writer.

Lawrence's success in describing the life of external things was the result of a force of awareness, a genius of awareness, in himself. But it had its limitations. The very intensity of his intuition, its demonic quality, kept him, when he went deeper than rabbits or places and tried to describe human beings, from seeing them except as examples of his own emotional problems. His characters lack the salt of objectivity. Further, in describing men and women he tried to go too far down into the dark sources of consciousness. Seeking for the fundamental springs of personality, he got *below* personality. He went under the Plimsoll line of identity. His novels are full of subtle human conflicts, but they are never conflicts which particularize his characters as human beings; they are examples of passions, of states of feeling, mostly in the abstract. His people, with one or two exceptions, are merely wells or rather geysers of instinct, acting from impulses so obscure that they dim, they don't illuminate, individuality. As a novelist, Lawrence's profound sensibility tended to defeat its own ends.

Yet this emphasis on the inner reality, the reality below consciousness and below will, was also one of the strengths of Lawrence, even if it sometimes got in his way. For Lawrence was right; there *is* a dark core of being, 'there *is* a flame or a Life Everlasting wreathing through the cosmos for ever and giving us our renewal, once we can get in touch with it'. Knowing that may not be of use in constructing novels, which are as much concerned with the social man as they are with the essence of man's being, but such knowledge gives the knower a sense of reality, and anyone who has it is worth listening to. And for this reason Lawrence, with all his wordiness, his *longueurs,* his digressions, is worth listening to. Even when he is off the track, as in the long essay on Hardy in the present volume, he is worth listening to. That is why it is a reproach to our decade that we can say it has left Lawrence to one side.

The Saturday Review, October 31, 1936.

DAVID GARNETT (1892-   )

... the man with most creative energy that I remember was D. H. Lawrence, whom I knew well between 1912 and the spring of 1915. His creative powers were perhaps then at their greatest, though they can never have slackened very much. A reference to the list of his works shows that he wrote thirty volumes or so in about eighteen years, besides travelling all over the world and living an astonishingly full life. When I knew him Lawrence would write perfectly happily while he was cooking a meal with several idle people sky-larking in the same room. Sitting curiously hunched up on a stool with his head a bit on one side he would scratch away in a foreign exercise book, dipping a bad pen in a penny bottle of ink, pause to scratch his head with the pen-holder, scratch down another sentence, rise and squint at the spaghetti, and subside to scratch more sentences on to the paper until we stopped his work with questions, or with affectionate horse-play, or until he called us to eat the meal that he had cooked. In those days his writing was an occupation that filled all the corners of his spare time but which was never allowed to interfere with his seeing fresh people, or with all-day excursions to gather plants for my herbarium. No doubt it was not always so, but that it should have ever been is astonishing to me, for I have never known another writer who could work under anything like such conditions. What Lawrence had to say poured out of him, and if he did not get it right the first time he repeated himself like a thrush singing, until the point was hammered in. I do not think he found it at all easy to go over what he had written, or to remould and reshape his work. If it just had to be done, no doubt he would do it, for he was never a shirker, but I believe he would always have found it much easier to write a new version. For the most part, I have the impression that he was satisfied with the first draft. He was an artist and a poet, but he could not grind away the corners to achieve perfection. Moreover, I believe it was always a relief to him to stop being an artist, switch off all self-criticism, and become the prophet. For what a prophet writes never has to be scrapped; the darker and more dogmatic it is the better many people will like it.

A volume of Lawrence's essays, travel sketches, reviews of books, etc., many of which have never been printed before, and running to over eight hundred pages, has just been published under the title *Phoenix*. It has inevitably a resemblance to the family rag-basket, for just as there are shreds in that which provide vivid reminders of all the frocks the daughters of the family have worn in the last twenty years, so *Phoenix* provides samples of Lawrence's development as a writer, as an artist and as a thinker, at all stages of his life. My own preference is so strongly for the early Lawrence whom I knew, that my judgments will no doubt seem prejudiced to many of his admirers. It is true that there is no firm dividing line in Lawrence's life: that he began writing awful unreadable stuff like that about the lion and the unicorn fighting for the crown, published in Murry's booklets called *The Signature*, quite early, and that he wrote lovely stories quite at the end of his life. But there was a sort of turning point marked by his growing a beard. In the days before the beard, Lawrence was always eager, alive, sometimes petulant and scolding, but then laughing and ragging himself and his own petulance. The beard marked a willingness to surrender himself to the prophet; he concealed himself in the beard and lost the will to mock at himself and to criticize himself. Not that it was all his fault—he was shamefully treated during and after the war—the worms turned on him and he grew a bit savage. A lot of the prophetic writing is like the snarling of a dog that has been chained up and tormented. And he took the war personally, not as the suffering of millions of men, but as though it had been aimed, somehow, particularly at him.

It is therefore with delight that one opens *Phoenix* on the *Whistling of Birds* ... The artist and the preacher in Lawrence are blended in a poetic harmony in this lovely little sermon, which tells how, on the first sign of thaw, the doves began to coo and the blackbirds to whistle.

Surely the call is premature while the clods are still frozen and the ground is littered with the remains of wings! Yet we have no choice. In the bottoms of impenetrable blackthorn, each evening and morning now, out flickers a whistling of birds. Where does it come from, the song? After so long a cruelty, how can they make it up so quickly? But it bubbles through them, they are like little wellheads, little fountain-heads whence the spring trickles and bubbles forth. It is not of their own doing. In their throats the new life distils itself into sound. It is the rising of silvery sap of a new summer, gurgling itself forth.

And after the sermon cleansing one's heart of the suffering of the war, are two lovely reminiscences of two pets with which the Lawrence children tormented their mother. *Adolph* was a wild tiny rabbit that their father brought home to them, and Lawrence has caught the rabbit-soul with intuitive understanding. While he was writing these pages, he became a rabbit himself, and explains from the inside the contradiction of the rabbit's terror and his jaunty, insulting defiance. And in the next sketch he gives an equally good portrait of a puppy. In Part II, *Peoples, Countries, Races,* there are delightful impressions of Lawrence's first visit to Germany: of a French barber in Metz, of a hailstorm in the Rhineland and of wayside Christs in the Tirol, which he described also in one of the sketches in the volume *Love Among the Haystacks* and then of Indians drumming and dancing, and of the Nottingham mining countryside.

In Part III, *Love and Sex,* there isn't very much matter that is new to us. Indeed, one of the essays, 'Women are so Cocksure', which Mr E. D. McDonald tells us is unpublished, I believe I have seen somewhere, in print. The excellent essay on 'Pornography and Obscenity' is reprinted here. The weakness of Lawrence's intuitive, dogmatic moralizing is well illustrated in 'Making Love to Music', an essay on modern dancing. If the couples in the ballrooms had been Mexicans or Indians how he would have worshipped just what he denounces here. Lawrence didn't dance himself. Most of these essays on *Love and Sex,* which will be read as a great revelation of truth, are just Primitive Methodist stuff that would go down equally well at a Revival meeting. Part IV, *Literature and Art,* is more interesting (to me at all events): a mixup of prefaces to his own and other people's books and reviews, some really good and some only saucy, but all of them worth reading and full of the lively mockery of his mind. The long study of Thomas Hardy

I haven't read. There is an attack on Galsworthy and a swipe, in a bad temper, at Cunninghame Graham and Van Vechten's *Nigger Heaven* is wiped out for ever. In an introduction to a Bibliography of his own books by Mr McDonald he says: 'I have never read one of my own published works.' The awful thing is that this piece of swank was really true, and the reason was that Lawrence was running away from himself all his life. The artist did not want to have to face that he had only daubed in his masterpieces. No doubt the tubercle germ must be held responsible. But one wonders what Lawrence would have been like without the germ burning him up faster than ordinary men. Could he have plodded patiently and worked in cold blood without the fever? But how well he hits things off in sentences. Shestov's style with all the conjunctions clipped out of it is 'like a man with no buttons on his clothes'. Part V is a long essay on *Education of the People* which I could not get on with at all. Part VI, *Ethics, Psychology, Philosophy,* is mostly the sort of stuff I dislike. For example, two unfinished essays about the Duc de Lauzun, 'who belongs to the fag-end of the French brocade period', whose faults he attributes to reading Restif de la Bretonne when he was a boy—ten years or so before Restif wrote anything, and twenty years before *Les Contemporaines*. Part VII has a fragment of a novel which starts horribly with a lot of falsity about an old country house and an ancient family and then bursts into passages of lyrical beauty—Lawrence at his very best—describing the fish following the boat on which the sick man is sailing home. And there is an unfinished fragment of a novel about the future which starts like Hudson's *A Crystal Age*. *Phoenix* is a most important addition to the collection of Lawrence's writings.

The New Statesman and Nation, November 21, 1936.

W. H. AUDEN (1907-   )

(SOME NOTES ON D. H. LAWRENCE)

There is one characteristic of D. H. Lawrence which can never fail to delight the reader, namely, the enormous pleasure he took in writing. Superficially the voice may be strident, hectoring, even, in his deplorable letters (as dreadful as Rilke's), self-pitying, but *au fond*—what wonderful high spirits! How can the class take their wigging quite seriously when teacher is having such fun giving it?

... There are four things which Lawrence does supremely well: writing about non-human nature, writing as a stranger about places and people he sees for the first time, criticizing books, and describing states of irrational hostility between man and man or man and woman.

In my opinion, the poems in *Birds, Beasts, and Flowers* are Lawrence's greatest achievement. To begin with, they are of great technical interest: so far as I know, Lawrence is the only poet on whom

Whitman has had a fruitful influence; his free verse is quite new, but without Whitman it could not have been written. Then, whenever he writes about animals or plants, the anger and frustration which too often intrude in his descriptions of human beings vanish, *agape* takes their place, and the joy of vision is equal to the joy in writing. To Wordsworth the creatures are symbols of great mysterious powers; to the naturalist, examples of a beautiful or interesting species to be observed objectively; Lawrence, on the other hand, loves them neither as numinous symbols nor as aesthetic objects but as neighbours. To a fig tree or a tortoise he gives that passionate personal attention usually offered by lonely or shy people, or by children, invalids, prisoners, and the like; the others are too busy, too accustomed to having their own way. (The forerunner of these poems is Christopher Smart's description of his cat Jeffrey in 'Jubilate Agno,' which he wrote in an asylum.)

All the travel books—*Twilight in Italy, Sea and Sardinia,* and so on—are excellent. Here again Lawrence has the intensity of the lonely man looking in at a life which is not his and trying to guess what it is really like. In a way he would like to be invited to join in, but in his heart of hearts he knows that would be a fatal disappointment.

Lawrence's literary criticism *Studies in Classical American Literature,* the essay on 'Galsworthy', the reviews of novels—are wonderful in a very odd way ... He is often quite dotty, he does not make the faintest pretence at being objective, but he is so passionately interested in the work he is talking about and so little interested in his reputation as a critic that even when he is violently and quite unfairly attacking an author, he makes him sound far more exciting and worth reading than most critics make one sound whom they are professing to praise. I shall never forget my disappointment when, having just finished Lawrence's essay on him, I rushed off to read the novels of Fenimore Cooper.

Like Blake, Lawrence was interested, not in 'individuals', but in 'states'. In writing about nature or about strangers this does not matter, as these are only experienced as states of being, but it is a serious drawback in writing fiction which cannot avoid the individual and his relations to other individuals over a stretch of time. Lawrence is never at ease when the time is a long one, so that none of his long novels quite succeeds because we get bored with the lack of a character to bind the states together and give them uniqueness. With his Righteous Man and his Righteous Woman he flops utterly. Mellors is as intolerable as Uncle Tom.

Lawrence is now neglected as an artist because his *kerygma* no longer seems good news; yet the situation from which he tried to save us is too little changed and too desperate for us to read him as a classic whose theories, like Dante's views of the relation between pope and emperor, belong to history. A sick patient cannot take a detached view of the bedside manners of a doctor who has failed to cure him.

Lawrence is best regarded as a Christian heretic. Like Nietzsche and unlike Goethe, who was simply unchristian, Lawrence was obsessed with Christianity, and it seems as inevitable that his last finished work should have been *The Man Who Died* as that Nietzsche should have ended by signing himself The Crucified. (Goethe thought the Cross in such bad taste.)

Heresies usually go in pairs. A half-truth which becomes a lie by claiming to express the whole dogma provokes the opposite half-truth to a similar excess. Further, at any particular period it is usually one particular dogma that is most liable to heretical distortion. In the fourth and seventeenth centuries, for example, the main issue was nature and grace—that is, men were concerned with the First Person of the Trinity. The characteristic debate of the twentieth century as of the second is over Christology.

It is not the relation of free will to determinism but of the Word to the flesh, the universal to the individual, the eternal to the historical, which seems to our generation the real problem involving our liberty and happiness.

Lawrence's life and work was a violent crusade against the liberal bourgeois perversion of Christianity according to which:

1. The mind is spiritual. The body is base.

2. White-collar work is respectable. Manual labour is 'low'.

3. True love between the sexes is the marriage of two minds. The physical relation between their bodies is an unfortunate necessity, a rather ugly greed justifiable only as a means to begetting children.

4. The flesh cannot be redeemed. It can only be kept quiet by repression or indulgence while the mind pursues its salvation.

5. Utopia will be a society in which, thanks to the progress of science, the production of goods has become so ample and so automatic that the flesh has ceased to be a problem. There will be no need of a coercive authority, and every citizen will be able to devote his whole time to contemplation and culture.

In so far as these attitudes claim to be Christian, they imply a Gnostic conception of the Incarnation. The Word was not mere historical flesh but briefly appeared in borrowed flesh to teach men, not how to redeem their flesh and their time, but how to redeem their minds from flesh and time.

In reaction Lawrence preached the opposite:

1. The body is good. The mind is corrupt.

2. Nearly all intellectual and white-collar work is mechanical and sterile. Manual labour when it is really manual and not just machine-minding is free and creative.

3. True love between the sexes is a creation of the Dark God, the phys-

ical sympathy of two bodies. Spiritual intimacy is always hostile to this.

4. The instinctive flesh must redeem the corrupt mind.

5. Salvation for society is probably impossible, but if it should come to pass, it will be through the authority of an instinctive genius.

This is the same gnosticism stood on its head. The Word is not made flesh for the true Word *is* the flesh. Lawrence's Christ is the pre-Adamic hero who rescues Adam and Eve from their bondage in the White Devil of mechanical reason and reflective consciousness.

Lawrence is right in attacking the intellectual who forgets that all genuine thinking has its roots in passion, but the cure he suggests, to retreat from desire to passion, is dangerously wrong. It is not accidental that *The Plumed Serpent* should emit such an unpleasant whiff of fascism, for fascism gives the same answer to the same Cartesian errors, only on a mass scale instead of a personal one. Accordingly it makes political passion supreme and dismisses personal feeling as cavalierly as Lawrence did the reverse.

As against a mechanical history of the spirit which ignores man as a natural creature and rushes him helplessly, blindly forward, Lawrence is right in reasserting natural time with its recurrent rhythms, but in so far as he makes natural time the only real time his attitude towards human history and social life remains purely negative, and the only people who are in a position to lead, even approximately, the life of which he approves are *rentiers* or artists or gipsies with passports. For his opponents time is an abstract concept of history in which there is no real present; for Lawrence time is a succession of passionate present moments for which past and future have no meaning.

'Sex isn't sin . . . until the dirty mind pokes in.' Exactly. And for that reason it is impossible to preach about purity, for to say 'you mustn't think about sex' has the same effect as saying 'you may think about anything you like except elephants'. By its very nature art is an act of making experience conscious, which means that it cannot and must not try to deal with any experience which is 'existential', that is, is falsified by reflection. *Lady Chatterley's Lover* is, unfortunately, as pornographic as *Fanny Hill*. It is of necessity as indecent as, at the other end of the psycho-somatic scale, must be all attempts to describe the Beatific Vision.

As far as one can judge, Lawrence was by temperament monogamous. The average man is not, and on him the effect of reading Lawrence has been, only too often, to send him (or her) off in a search for the perfect sleeping partner who, according to the doctrine, is most likely to be found among 'primitive' or working-class types, one, in fact, who is, outside of the bed, an awful bore. By always presenting the 'white' spiritual love and the love of the 'Dark' God as irreconcilable enemies, Lawrence has encouraged people in fact—though not of course in intention—to divide their lives between 'white' relations and 'dark'. This is to deny the possibility of a happy marriage, for, however difficult to achieve, marriage is by definition a reconciliation of the two.

For a complete life a man requires six kinds of love—for his wife, for his children, for his friends, for his neighbours, for his work, and for God. In our time the secularization of belief, the mechanization of work, the atomization of society, birth control, and so on tend to deprive him of all but the first. If the average man today is obsessed with sex, it is partly because it seems to him the only sphere in which he is a free agent, in which his failures and his triumphs are really his; hence if he fails here, he has achieved nothing with his life. Lawrence was luckier than the majority because he had a second love, his work, but to judge from his books, even two loves are not enough, or, rather, it is too much of a strain on them to carry all the emotion due to the others.

Lawrence's answers do not mean much to us any more; his questions still disturb a good deal. His genuine visions of plants, of animals, of certain passionate states will be treasured even if and when all his questions and ours, being truly answered, have ceased to vex. . . .

First published in *The Nation,* April 26, 1947. © W. H. Auden.

Critics on D. H. Lawrence since 1950

ROGER DATALLER

Elements of D. H. Lawrence's Prose Style

I

...What the Heath was to Hardy, so was the Mine to Lawrence, imparting a focus, a swift bright order of sight, a swooping to the depths, a soaring into the sunlight, dichotomy peculiar to the Eastwood environment.

II

Interwoven with this intensely visual attitude, we mark the sense of touch, of handling things. For Lawrence—as for so many others of his class—home meant social obligation. There was bread to be baked (one might assist in that), boots and brasses to shine, toast and tea to make, socks to darn, floors to scrub. In the later Lawrence these evidences of self-reliance (he even turned to the making of furniture) are regarded quite erroneously as an idiosyncrasy of the artist, when indeed it was the heritage of his childhood. However wrong Lawrence went about other things his characters at work are entirely convincing. Virginia Woolf indicated the necessity of a room of one's own, a sanctum, where isolated from the stress of family life, a person could think creatively. But Lawrence is an example of the advantage of not having a room of one's own, of sharing in full the family life. One has only to compare, for instance, the account of the dinner given by Mrs Ramsay to her family and guests in *To the Lighthouse,* with a meal in one of Lawrence's novels—Lilly, for example, making tea for Aaron in *Aaron's Rod*—to realize that Mrs Ramsay's relation to the viands was only a vicarious one, the real preparation and pride of accomplishment being with the maid behind the scenes, whereas, even in the act of making tea with Lawrence, we share the scene in a directly conveyed experience. Mrs Woolf, for all her sensibility, was the prisoner of her own economic independence. An element of scarcity intensifies value. Consider the care with which Mrs Morel spends a few pence upon a flowered dish, and the pleasure that its simple decoration brings to herself and Paul. To Virginia Woolf, domestic work was a burden. (She would claim that being unable to cut up butcher's meat efficiently, it was far better for her to stick to her writing.) To Lawrence, these presumably commonplace tasks were the warp and woof of experience. How deeply implanted this necessity was we find in his essay on *The Education of the People:*

> From earliest childhood, let us have independence and self dependence. Every child to do all it can for itself, clean its own boots, brush and fold its own clothes, fetch and carry for itself, mend its own stockings, boy and girl alike, patch its own garments, and as soon as possible, make as well as mend for itself. Men and women are happy, and children the same.[1]

This, which at first hearing may seem like an echo from *Emile,* derives not from Rousseau at all, but from the springs of Eastwood life. 'Self dependence is independence.' He continues, 'To be free one must be self sufficient, particularly in small, material personal matters.' Then:

> The actual doing of things is in itself a joy. If I wash the dishes, I learn a quick, light touch of china and earthenware, the feel of it, the weight and roll and poise of it, the peculiar hotness, and quickness, or slowness of its surface. I am in the middle of an infinite complexity of motions and adjustments and quick apprehensive contacts. Nimble faculties hover and play along my nerves, the primal consciousness is alive in me.[2]

Here is the touchstone of Lawrence's style. Transformed into fiction it becomes impressive indeed, for in it we see the interfusing of intense sensibility with the concrete world, of the inner with the outer reality. It is this capacity, this intuitive integration of an 'infinite complexity of motions and adjustments' that imparts to Lawrence's work a finer, almost poetical, texture, so that when the normal occupations of cottage or farmhouse are indicated, we are conscious of meaning much deeper than would appear upon the surface. Take the episode in *The White Peacock,* when Lettie after her rejection of George, visits the farm on Christmas Eve, and shares the labour of making mincemeat. They are peeling apples. George is stoning raisins:

> She went to the table, and occupied one side with her apple peeling. George had not spoken to her. So she said:

[1] *Phoenix*, p. 649.   [2] *Phoenix*, p. 650.

'I won't help you George, because I don't like to feel my fingers so sticky, and because I love to see you so domesticated.'

'You'll enjoy the sight a long time, then, for these things are numberless.'

'You should eat one now and then—I always do.'

'If I ate one I should eat the lot.'

'Then you will give me your one.'

He passed her a handful without speaking.

'That is too many, your mother is looking. Let me just finish this apple. There, I've broken the peel!'

She swings the curling strip of peel, so that when it falls it may indicate the initials of her lover. The father, crudely humourous, suggests that it indicates G:

'George,' said Emily sharply, 'you're leaving nothing but the husks.' He too was angry.

'And he would fain fill his belly with the husks that the swine did eat,' he said quietly, taking a handful of the fruit that he had picked, and putting some in his mouth. Emily snatched away the basin. 'It's too bad,' she said.

'Here,' said Lettie, handing him an apple she had peeled.

'You may have an apple, greedy boy.'

He took it and looked at it. Then a malicious smile twinkled in his eyes—and he said:

'If you give me the apple, to whom will you give the peel?'

'The swine,' she said, as if she had only understood his first reference to the Prodigal Son. He put the apple on the table.

'Don't you want it?' she said.

'Mother,' he said comically, as if jesting, 'she is offering me the apple like Eve.'

Like a flash, she snatched the apple from him, hid it in her skirts a moment, looking at him with dilated eyes, and then she flung it in the fire. She missed, and her father leaned forward and picked it off the hob saying:

'The pigs may as well have it. You were slow, George—when a lady offers you a thing you don't have to make mouths.'[3]

The subtle undertones of this passage, in which the whole theme of *The White Peacock* is displayed, are worthy of the closest consideration; the concentration of fact and symbol, the emotional tension of the Lettie-George relationship revealed in casual, almost flippant conversation, yet pregnant as a poem. Without the stoning of the raisins, the peeling of the apples, where would it be?

No less significant, and much more closely identified with Lawrence's early domestic training is the incident in *Sons and Lovers*,

---

[3] *The White Peacock*, pp. 103–5.

when Mrs Morel, visiting the market, leaves the bread in the oven to
be attended to by Paul. Miriam and Beatrice enter. Beatrice, a lively
piece, to Miriam's constrained disgust, rags the not unresponsive Paul.
He lights his cigarette at that of Beatrice, 'his eyes trembling with
mischief, and his full, almost sensual mouth quivering', and Beatrice
gives him a little kiss on the cheek. But they have quite forgotten the
bread.

> 'By Jove,' he cried, flinging open the oven door.
> Out puffed the bluish smoke and a smell of burnt bread.
> 'Oh, golly!' cried Beatrice, coming to his side. He crouched before
> the oven, and she peered over his shoulder. 'This is what comes of
> the oblivion of love, my boy.'
> Paul was ruefully removing the loaves. One was burnt black on the
> hot side; another was as hard as a brick. He set the doors open to
> blow away the smell of burned bread. Beatrice grated away, puffing
> her cigarette, knocking the charcoal off the poor loaf.
> 'My word, Miriam! you're in for it this time,' said Beatrice.
> 'I?' exclaimed Miriam in amazement.
> 'You'd better be gone when his mother comes in. I know why King
> Alfred burned the cakes. . . .'

Later, Paul surveys the burnt loaf sadly:

> 'It's a mess,' he said.
> 'But,' answered Miriam impatiently, 'what is it, after all—twopence
> ha'penny.'
> 'Yes, but it's the mater's precious baking, and she'll take it to heart.
> However, it's no good bothering.'

So Mrs Morel returns, and discovers the offending loaf:

> 'I forgot the bread, mother,' he said.
> There was no answer from the other woman.
> 'Well,' he said, 'it's only twopence ha'penny. I can pay you for that.'
> Being angry, he put three pennies on the table, and slid them to-
> wards his mother. She turned away her head. Her mouth was shut
> tightly.[4]

A moment or two later she announces that she knows why the bread
was spoilt—because, of course, he had been engrossed with Miriam!
The primal pride of a working class housewife's baking, the prerequisite of all, her bread, and the profound annoyance that this should
have been spoilt, is interwoven with the Miriam issue. Paul has committed the almost unforgivable sin, that of charcoaled bread, and
united with this is the unforgivable Miriam intrusion. And even more
subtly, Miriam's suggestion that the loaf is worth not more than two-

[4] *Sons and Lovers*, pp. 206–10.

pence halfpenny, as though the payment of money could wipe out the disaster that has come upon them. It is Miriam's contemptuous two-pence halfpenny—tendered by Paul—that is rejected, and we are not surprised when this leads to her rejection in the poignantly moving scene that follows.

Discussing the relationship of Tom Brangwen and the child Anna in *The Rainbow*, Dr F. R. Leavis has compared the associational values of D. H. Lawrence's work with those of George Eliot, the peculiar quality that makes Lawrence's writing more compulsive than hers. 'Nor could she have evoked with that sensuous immediacy the change to the wet night ("The child was suddenly still, shocked, finding the rain on its face and the darkness") and then to the other world of the lantern-lit and warm-smelling barn, full of the tranquillizing wonder of its strangeness, when Brangwen goes with the child in his arms to feed the cows.'[5] Part of that sensuous immediacy, was not only in terms of 'mother', 'shawl', 'chapel', as Dr Leavis indicates, but also from the habit of doing things. Carrying fodder to stabled cattle (Lawrence must have done this often at the Haggs) involves a slight trickle of chop from the pan—for one always tends to overload—a detail of narrative that could only have been inserted by one who had performed the operation. So Tom spills the fodder. He rests the pan on the manger before tilting (one always does that), and when the task is done sits for a moment or two on the box in the calmly breathing peace of the stable, listening to the snuffing of the animals and the ripple of links through the tethering ring.

Within this field of integrated sensibility, Lawrence is superb. He fails only when he essays a situation completely alien to his own experience, as in the case of Birkin driving a motor car (in *Women in Love*) by night, through unfamiliar roads in Sherwood Forest:

> He sat still like an Egyptian Pharaoh, driving the car. He felt as if he were seated in immemorial potency, like the great carven statues of real Egypt, as real and as fulfilled with subtle strength, as these are, with a vague inscrutable smile on the lips. . . . They ran on in silence. But with a sort of second consciousness he steered the car towards a destination.[6]

The integration here is false. Lawrence never drove a car. It is obvious that he had never driven a car by night in Sherwood Forest. One doesn't steer by headlights down leafy tracks and lanes 'with a sort of second consciousness'. It can't be done, not even by resuscitated, subtly smiling Pharaohs. Lawrence retained the customary impression of the non-driver, that handling a car by night involves merely the switching on of headlights, and the turning of a wheel.

---

[5] *Scrutiny*, Winter, 1951–52.
[6] *Women in Love*, p. 335.

More elaborately, the failure of Lawrence with unfamiliar material is set out in the many pages of *The Plumed Serpent*, where the assumption of ritualistic clothing, food, ablutions, becomes frankly a bore. Being what he was, he had to do the job thoroughly, pegging desperately with lifeless material. Adapted from Mexican folk-lore, *The Plumed Serpent* is a grafting on, an elaborate pastiche, a curiosity of creative endeavour, the grim warning of a hag-ridden thesis.

But Lawrence lapsed seldom. The true note is struck in the Lilly-Aaron relationship, the rubbing of the sick Aaron with oils 'as mothers do their babies', and the domestic economy of the little man:

> Lilly's skilful housewifery always irritated Aaron: it was so self-sufficient. But the most irritating of all was the little man's unconscious assumption of priority. Poor Lilly was actually unaware that he assumed this quiet predominance over others. He mashed the potatoes, he heated the plates, he warmed the red wine, he whisked the eggs into the milk pudding, and served his visitor like a housemaid ...
>
> At last the meal was ready. Lilly drew the curtains, switched off the central light, put the green shaded electric light on the table, and the two men drew up to the meal. It was good food, well cooked and hot. Certainly Lilly's hands were no longer clean: but it was clean dirt, as he said.[7]

'Clean dirt', the broad, but somehow subtle distinction of those who work with their hands.

Thus Lawrence is most himself, and consequently at his finest point as a creative artist, when intuitively his training, practically domestic, and Nonconformistly cultural, is at one with his subject. Towards the end of his life—from ill-health, and a greater necessity to call upon the services of others, passing as he did from one hotel to another, in an atmosphere of angry or baffled resignation (the period of *Pansies*)—the close texture of Lawrence's writing suffered. It became adulterated by stress of Apocalyptic purpose, though in the background, latent, as a luminous possibility, remained the primal master. About a year from the end he writes to one who knew him in the Eastwood days: 'Whatever I forget, I shall never forget the Haggs—I loved it so. I loved to come to you all, it really was a new life began in me there ... Tell your mother I never forget, no matter where life carries us ... Because whatever else I am, I am somewhere still the same Bert who rushed with such joy to the Haggs.'[8]

It was true, not only of the Haggs.

Essays in Criticism, Vol. III, No. 4, October 1953, pp. 416–24.

---

[7] *Aaron's Rod*, p. 112.
[8] *Letters*, pp. 761–2.

T. B. TOMLINSON

Lawrence and Modern Life:
Sons and Lovers, Women in Love

The most telling criticism of *Women in Love* has been that it is the climax of a literary career expressing distrust in, and finally disgust with, modern life. I don't myself believe this to be true, but those who do would add that it is not just 'modern' life, or our mechanistic civilization, that Lawrence distrusts, but humanity itself. Thus Gerald's delight in choking Gudrun, at the end of *Women in Love*, is prefigured in for instance, 'The Prussian Officer', in Paul Morel's treatment of Miriam, and in the twisted view of love that these stories seem to entail. On this reading the whole business is summed up in Birkin's solipsistic *contemptus mundi*; which, moreover, is literally 'contempt' since it appears to look forward to nothing beyond the mechanistic Darwinian hope that the 'creative mystery' will throw up new and 'higher' forms of life than man. The following, for instance, seems to me convincing in context, but one can easily see the sense in which it might be worrying:

> 'The whole idea is dead. Humanity itself is dry-rotten, really. There are myriads of human beings hanging on the bush—and they look very nice and rosy, your healthy young men and women. But they are apples of Sodom, as a matter of fact, Dead Sea Fruit, gall-apples. It isn't true that they have any significance—their insides are full of bitter, corrupt ash.'

It is clear that Lawrence was indeed tempted by a deep distrust in human life; and moreover it is precisely this insecurity that is behind the over-insistent, precious note in his worst prose:

> It was a perfect passing away for both of them, and at the same time the most intolerable accession into being, the marvellous fullness of immediate gratification, overwhelming, outflooding from the source of the deepest life-force, the darkest, deepest, strangest life-source of the human body, at the back and base of the loins.

The bathos of this can't possibly be dismissed as a mere lapse of 'style' or 'artistry'. Lawrence here is trying so hard to replace something that he feels has gone from human life that the result, though obviously sincerely meant, is flat and literal-minded. It is in passages like this, from 'Excurse' in *Women in Love*, that the real charge against

Lawrence comes to a head: he is a man pretending to vitalism, but actually despairing; and despairing not only to the point where, for him and Birkin, 'Humanity is a huge aggregate lie', but to the point where in consequence his own prose becomes a mere flailing about, a desperate search that achieves only a literal-minded parody of the poetic insight he can command elsewhere.

Part of the difficulty in answering this very real charge against Lawrence is and always has been that the charge itself is seldom properly made. It is in the air in all Lawrence discussions and in most of the critical work on him; but too often a fear of the *immediacy* in all Lawrence's prose (whether good or bad) forces people into evasive tactics that twist the charge into forms that are cruder and easier to deal with. As a result of this, the suggested answers tend to be either partial or, at times, completely wide of the mark. For instance, one of the most influential and representative books recently has been Eliseo Vivas's *D. H. Lawrence: The Failure and Triumph of Art* (Northwestern, 1960). Professor Vivas raises essential criticisms of the Laurentian ethic and personality forcibly, but in such a form as to emasculate them, render them inapplicable to what he calls 'pure art'. Characteristically, Vivas will state that evidence from Lawrence's biographers or acquaintances (e.g. of his alleged cowardice and fear of women) is irrelevant to a consideration of art; and *then* go on to report the incident from 'life': 'Whether Lawrence was a physical coward or not is not here in question. That he was a physical bully, we know. The story Knud Merrild tells about the beating Lawrence gave the dog is enough evidence. But whatever the case, his heroes are not "men" in the sense in which a marine sergeant or a Spanish-American would use the term.'

That is an *argumentum ad hominem* if ever there was one, particularly since there are no qualifications following in Vivas's text. He moves straight on to another section (section 5 of Chapter VII) on 'The Prussian Officer'. I think that Vivas's case against the 'corrosive emotion' evident in parts at least of 'The Prussian Officer' is a strong one. But seeing the dangers in that story, how could he not have had second thoughts about the relevance of the kind of 'men' instanced in 'a marine sergeant or a Spanish-American'?

But that muddling of literary criticism and biography, or alleged biography, is particularly common in Lawrence studies. Like many people today, Vivas seems fascinated by Lawrence, but at the same time unable to face steadily certain tendencies in Lawrence's life and art. The uncontrolled abuse that he accords Lawrence's 'propaganda' in stories like *Aaron's Rod*, for instance, again distorts what might have been a valid criticism: 'But the novel is a didactic tract, and as such it calls for the comment that it is an expression of Lawrence's unmitigated, immature, foot-stamping, table-pounding, fretting, pouting, cry-baby, petulant, selfishness—a sheer, uncomplicated, unrestrained, colossally arrogant, self-centred selfishness.' This passage betrays an irritation against Lawrence, and a fear of him, that spread beyond the single case of *Aaron's Rod*. (The obsessively repetitive adjectives alone indicate an instinctive response stronger than the apparent occasion for them, a single novel.) In part this is a genuine fear, truly based: when Lawrence's own prose disintegrates, it generally does so in ways that reveal something to be afraid *of*, a fiercely destructive urge that is rarely absent from his work. Where Vivas and a good many others go wrong, however, is in not meeting this difficulty: they reduce it to something easily discussible—Lawrence's biography, or his 'propaganda', or his 'style'—and attempt to show how these things are irrelevant to his 'art'. One of the most unfortunate results of this is to place Lawrence on a pedestal where, in the end, *no* criticism can touch him . . .

The crucial case in any assessment of Lawrence, or in any adverse criticism of him, is *Women in Love*. But the beginnings of a possible answer to basic criticisms of his novels, and of his view of modern life, seem to me best sought in a consideration of some aspects of *Sons and Lovers*: in particular, the part Walter Morel has to play there. In his account of Lawrence Vivas—and again he is representative—is worried by scenes like the Morels' kitchen fight in Chapter I of *Sons and Lovers*. He admires the 'immediacy' of the writing, but criticizes the scene, as I understand him, on two grounds. First, he complains that the 'experience of being dragged into the quarrel is anything but pleasant and it induces in the reader ugly and frustrated emotions which he could well do without'. Second—and this is a very common complaint about *Sons and Lovers*—he feels Lawrence is unfairly a partisan in the fight: ' . . . Lawrence himself is on the side of the young wife against the drunken husband . . . Lawrence here is not merely presenting a quarrel but is doing more, he is probably justifying a private grudge of his own.' By this, I take it, Vivas means that Lawrence is indulging a grudge against his own father.

Both these objections seem to me to be based on a crucial misreading —a misreading not just of this scene but of *Sons and Lovers* as a whole and, through this, of Lawrence's whole position with regard to modern society. As I read them, this and allied scenes seem to me to present Walter Morel as an extraordinarily impressive and dignified man. It's not just that Lawrence, as everyone agrees, can render the scenes in the mining village very well. The writing goes far beyond mere realism to find, along with the brutishness in this working-class culture—almost part of it, in fact—a directness and physicality, a blind honesty of feeling that is or can be a sustaining force beyond the grasp of either Paul or Mrs Morel. In the novel this is, admittedly, a *blind* honesty and energy—that is Lawrence's criticism of it—but the point of the whole novel, or one of the main points, is that it nevertheless offers something that a cultivated, highly sophisticated life cannot.

Lawrence is not on Mrs Morel's side unequivocally at all. Certainly, her way of living tends towards an essential refinement and an educated intelligence beyond the miner's range—this is, of course, developed in later novels in terms of Birkin, Ursula, Gudrun and others. But one of the main points made by *Sons and Lovers* is Lawrence's strong sense of the loss consequent upon this gain. Morel's personality, his physical presence felt in the very texture of the writing, show a powerful energy that strives against sophisticated and civilized living, the basic physicality in man that must, whatever the cost and whatever the outcome, resist any attempt at refinement:

> 'Good gracious,' she cried, 'coming home in his drunkenness!'
> 'Comin' home in his what?' he snarled, his hat over his eye.
> Suddenly her blood rose in a jet.
> 'Say you're *not* drunk!' she flashed.
> She had put down her saucepan, and was stirring the sugar into the beer. He dropped his two hands heavily on the table, and thrust his face forward at her.
> 'Say you're not drunk,' he repeated. 'Why, nobody but a nasty little bitch like you 'ud 'ave such a thought.'

This is indeed—Vivas is right—an ugly scene, and Morel is ugly in it ... But these are not emotions which a reader 'could well do without'. The scene is radically unsettling because it is cast in extremely personal terms—what great novel isn't at points?—and they cut pretty close to the bone. But an essential part of this unsettling quality is, quite simply, the tragedy of the man. His dignity, and the dignity of the life that produced him, is there in the scene in Chapter VIII where he undresses and—as Paul could never do—washes himself in the scullery and in front of the kitchen fire with a consciousness of himself that is entirely unembarrassing because it is unaffected. More impressively still, it is there in the scenes where he hears of William's death and helps bring the coffin into the cottage ... Paul's consciousness in these scenes is one of the key things about them; but another is an element of which he is only partly aware, sometimes not at all. The novel presents Walter as Paul's enemy, but also as representing, taking part in, a whole way of life that is both simpler and stronger than his, because less inquiring, less self-conscious:

> Paul saw drops of sweat fall from his father's brow. Six men were in the room—six coatless men, with yielding, struggling limbs, filling the room and knocking against the furniture. The coffin veered, and was gently lowered on to the chairs. The sweat fell from Morel's face on its boards.

In these scenes after William's death—at the pit-head and in the cottage—Walter is almost completely inarticulate, but they belong to him rather than to anybody else, and the spare directness of the writing focuses on him consistently.

It is precisely the unsophisticated dignity about the man that produces—because it *has* to—the sensual outbursts in scenes like the kitchen fight. In everything he is and does, Walter embodies a way of life that is valuable but also extremely vulnerable, and vulnerable in particular to the probing, intellectually-based advance that Paul is drawn to. Even in that scene, however, one is surely aware that the nature and interests of a man like Paul could easily combine to produce a refinement of cruelty that Walter is quite incapable of. Walter's cruelty is physical and immediate, brutish. Paul's more menacing cruelty later on is the product of a sensitive, reflecting intelligence, and the book shows Lawrence's deep concern that Paul's treatment of Miriam, for instance, or of his mother, is—has to be—far less human that Walter's reactions to his wife ever were.

The treatment of Baxter Dawes in *Sons and Lovers* is another crucial case, and, when put together with the treatment of Walter Morel, it forces one to the conclusion that even Lawrence's own statement, 'I shan't write in the same manner as *Sons and Lovers* again', may be slightly misleading. He didn't, of course, write in the same manner again, but there is surely a sense in which the distinctively working-class culture of Morel, Dawes, Clara, the Nottingham factory, together with the ways in which this culture and these people faced a new situation, is both important in its own right and remained important to Lawrence throughout his life. Dawes himself might seem an insignificant example, but in context he is not. Like Morel, Dawes is presented as a man defeated and humbled by Paul's sophistication (compare the scene where, in front of the other miners in the kitchen, Morel has to ask his son to count the butties' money for them). But like Morel too, Baxter has something about him that is instinctively surer, more self-contained, than anything or anybody in the more sophisticated later generation. Clara sees this, and it leads her to a realization that Dawes loved her in a way that Paul never could. There is a real truth in her emotional outburst, 'He loved me a thousand times better than you ever did ... He did! At any rate, he did respect me, and that's what you don't do.' In Paul she detects, correctly, a chilling reserve of critical intelligence, 'a sort of detached criticism of herself, a coldness' that fights off real respect. Baxter is more open. He can be, and is, brutal, but the resilience in the writing that gives us his brutality, or the brutality in the Morel's kitchen fight, is, if not exactly the men's own, then something with which they, rather than Paul or Mrs Morel, are immediately and instinctively in touch. It is this *instinctive* strength, too, that enables both Walter and Baxter Dawes to 'own themselves beaten', and Lawrence's rendering of their final defeat is in no sense patronizing or vindictive:

Dawes had been driven to the extremity of life, until he was afraid. He could go to the brink of death, he could lie on the edge and look in. Then, cowed, afraid, he had to crawl back, and like a beggar take what offered. There was a certain nobility in it. As Clara saw, he owned himself beaten, and he wanted to be taken back whether or not.

Women in Love offers no direct comparison with *Sons and Lovers*. The life figured in Walter Morel and Baxter Dawes is still relevant to Lawrence's concerns here—for instance it has a distinct impact on Ursula and Gudrun in the opening pages, and then later on as they see the labourers after the Arab mare incident, and later still as Gudrun thinks of the colliers when she is with Gerald under the railway bridge —but it is far off now, no longer available as a way of life that the major characters can either take part in or react strongly against. Nevertheless it seems to me that Gerald, the new colliery owner, is taken wrongly by most readers in something the same way as Walter Morel, and the very different life that he embodies, is taken wrongly. The two cases are related in that, if I am right about them, Lawrence's real interests and insights are more broadly based in modern life than they would be given any reading that concentrated on, say, Birkin's rejection of civilization and the sort of 'Benthamism' espoused by Skrebensky.

Because Gerald is not a Skrebensky at all. It's not just that Gerald is a person and Skrebensky, often, a mere symbol. Almost every key scene that features Gerald—the Arab mare, the water-party, the rabbit, 'Gladiatorial', the final death in the snow—has reserves of power and strength that cannot possibly be described as merely negative or corrupting. There is more to him, and about him, than merely the 'go' that first strikes the sisters (e.g. in the scene in 'Diver' where Gudrun gives the admittedly telling criticism of Gerald, 'The unfortunate thing is, where does his *go* go to, what becomes of it?'). And there is more to him than can adequately be described by seeing him as the centre for an adverse diagnosis, however keen and intelligent, of modern life. He is indeed, as Dr Leavis has shown, *the* centre for such a diagnosis; but in and around him there is in addition a force—the vague word will have to do for the moment—that escapes the diagnosis; that is not, in the very last analysis, susceptible to it.

If one asks, for instance, what it is that makes that final scene of Gerald's death so impressive, it is very hard to give an answer—much harder than it would be if Gerald's purpose in life, or lack of purpose, could be defined as Skrebensky's can. The actual breakdown of Skrebensky in front of Ursula is movingly rendered; but the issues at stake there, of his failure as a person and the related failure of his Benthamite philosophy of life, are relatively easy to grasp. This is not:

He was weak, but he did not want to rest, he wanted to go on and on to the end. Never again to stay, till he came to the end, that was all the desire that remained to him. So he drifted on and on, unconscious and weak, not thinking of anything, so long as he could keep in action.

The twilight spread a weird, unearthly light overhead, bluish-rose in colour, the cold blue night sank on the snow. In the valley below, behind, in the great bed of snow, were two small figures; Gudrun dropped on her knees, like one executed, and Loerke sitting propped near her. That was all.

In the first place it is odd, but I think utterly convincing, that the scene as a whole should begin with that drily witty remark of Loerke's as Gerald is desperately choking Gudrun (it follows the picture of Gudrun's ugly, swollen face with the eyes rolled back): 'Monsieur! ... Quand vous aurez fini—' It is this dry detachment of Loerke's—not in itself particularly admirable—that stops Gerald. And then, in that very sure change of key as Gerald goes off, one realizes that this scene might be as much an opening out of possibilities as a shutting down (though obviously it is that too). Gudrun, Gerald, Loerke—they all three of them resist definition, more strongly as a matter of fact than Birkin does. As far as Gerald is concerned, what we have here is a sense of his movement as at once a 'drifting' (his connections with the world and Gudrun and the mines have been snapped completely) and also a movement that is strongly individual, in a sense purposeful.

During the course of the novel the question of what strong attraction it is that binds Birkin to Gerald is kept tactfully unspecific ('Gladiatorial', for instance, explores the possibilities in physical contact between the two men without ever becoming summarizable as a chapter on 'homosexuality'). And here too, at the end, the question is left open, even while one central point is being made unambiguously clear: Gerald is, and has been all along, a centre for Birkin. Gerald has long ago shown that something in him cannot accept Birkin's Blutbrüderschaft; but even after this rejection, his presence in the book has been such as to offer stability to Birkin. His physical strength and skill, as in the tobogganing scenes just before his death, are one manifestation of this for Birkin as they are also for Gudrun (Gerald is 'one perfect line of force ...'); so even is his power as an industrial magnate:

> She [Gudrun] knew that if he were confronted with any problem, and hard actual difficulty, he would overcome it. If he laid hold of any idea, he would carry it through. He had the faculty of making order out of confusion. Only let him grip hold of a situation, and he would bring to pass an inevitable conclusion.

The criticisms of this force of 'will' are instantly felt and made by Gudrun, as they are by Birkin. But the force of even their criticisms spends itself before it has completely comprehended—let alone annulled—the 'perfect line of force' that Gerald can be. This is the real explanation for Birkin's stunned dismay at Gerald's death. Or to put the whole issue another way round: for all that has to be said against him, Gerald remains, up to and including the scene of his death, an implicit criticism of Birkin—especially, that is, of Birkin's deliberate choice in throwing the world away. I am not sure that the novel stresses this criticism of Birkin quite strongly enough; but it is, surely, more strongly made in terms of Gerald's abilities, and his physical presence, than in anything Ursula says in her early mocking irony at Birkin's expense. Hers is a negative position; Gerald's is not, or not entirely.

The part he plays in the snow scene at the end is certainly far from ineffectual or negative. Nor is his death entirely a matter of any 'tragic' loss of potential. The 'cold blue night', the great bed of snow, the 'fallen masses of rock and veins of snow slashing in and about the blackness of rock, veins of snow slashing vaguely in and about the blackness of rock'—all this, so far from merely symbolizing 'negation', is tangibly, physically present. Its presence is that of something at once compellingly ordered, and at the same time threateningly disordered ('veins of snow slashing in and about the blackness of rock.') And it belongs to Gerald, as of right. Indeed, all the snow scenes throughout 'Continental' and 'Snowed Up' are too strongly present to be either a mere antithesis of the African darkness or a mere illustration or dramatization of Gerald's personality. They effect a bewildering release of energies in everybody, as in the Schuhplatteln. But they are also something in the cosmos with which Gerald, above all, and with him Gudrun, are quite positively in touch:

> The passion came up in him, stroke after stroke, like the ringing of a bronze bell, so strong and unflawed and indomitable. His knees tightened to bronze as he hung above her soft face.... He felt strong as winter, his hands were living metal, invincible and not to be turned aside. His heart rang like a bell clanging inside him.

The danger of this state in Gerald is registered immediately in Gudrun's withdrawal, and later in the horror she feels when she sees his reflection in the mirror and cannot turn round to face him. But there is also here a still remaining sense that his energy is illimitable— something that could never, for instance, be contained or placed by any ironic vision like Loerke's—and it is this that makes his 'drifting' walk at the end a purposeful one. Though having said that, one has immediately to admit that the closing scene of Gerald's life is dominated by a quite terrifying sense of emptiness and loss ... but for all the criticisms the novel itself makes of Gerald and Gerald's way of life —or ways of life, since they are certainly various—he is also seen consistently as a stabilizing force. He is a centre against which Birkin's free inquiry is played off: until Gerald's death, when the prospect that faces Birkin is rendered, I think with absolute frankness on Lawrence's

E

part, as dismayingly problematical. Gerald's 'will' dominating the horse, brutally subduing the rabbit, diving for his sister, wrestling with Birkin—the manifestations of it are intensely rendered as well as various—is not merely 'understood' by Lawrence, but in some ways, and granted all the criticisms and qualifications, allowed its full value —almost, indeed, endorsed. Gerald did face the train and, at whatever cost, subdue the mare; and only Gerald, in the novel, could or would have done so. I am not suggesting that Gerald, or even Lawrence, is fully conscious of this role; only that it is there, and that its relevance to the modern world is of an active and positive kind.

Gerald Crich and Walter Morel: you could hardly pick two 'characters' less alike. But, as Dr Leavis has shown, more is at stake than any question of 'characterization', and the ways in which each of these men manifests a contained, baffled strength prove Lawrence's trust in life to be more widely and more truly based than any concentration on a Birkin philosophy of life could possibly do. As I have said, I think that both novels are currently misread, in so far as what these two men *are* is underestimated by most readers and critics. I also think that the *final* dimension Gerald has is underplayed even by Dr Leavis ... the cumulative tendency of his argument is to grant Birkin and Ursula a positive role denied to Gerald and Gudrun. For all the difficulties that face them, Birkin and Ursula are seen as testing out 'the need for some norm for the relations between men and women other than what Gerald and Gudrun enact'. They certainly do represent normative possibilities, and I would not for a moment deny the positive spirit in which the Birkin-Ursula relationship is shown. What I doubt is the implication that Gerald's life must in consequence be placed against Birkin's as essentially the negative one of the two...

The Critical Review, University of Melbourne, No. 8, 1965.

EDWARD ENGELBERG

Escape from the Circles of Experience: D. H. Lawrence's *The Rainbow* as a Modern *Bildungsroman*

I

Like all of Lawrence's novels, *The Rainbow* has suffered its share of abuse, but even admirers have attacked its ending—as they have that of *Sons and Lovers* and, to a lesser degree, *Women in Love*. This disaffection with the conclusions of novels otherwise highly regarded constitutes a serious charge: it calls in doubt not only the coherence of Lawrence's ideology but, more damaging, Lawrence's capacity as an artist to sustain his work and bring it to a proper end. With respect to *Sons and Lovers* and *The Rainbow* the question raised is the same: does the hero earn the rewards which the novelist bestows at the end? Or are Paul Morel's rather sudden determination to live purposefully and Ursula Brangwen's dramatic vision of the rainbow mere curtain-drops, the impatient gestures of a novelist already hurrying on to his next work? And what of Birkin's final disagreement with Ursula at the end of *Women in Love*—does it not sabotage the 'star equilibrium' toward which the novel seems to be shaped? It is difficult to defend the ending of *Sons and Lovers* without reservations; the conclusion to *Women in Love* is more defensible; but with *The Rainbow* the problem seems crucial: to call in doubt that novel's resolution is to question the structure and meaning of the whole book, and to undercut the vision of the rainbow is to undercut all that precedes it. The risks are so high because the structure of the novel and the meaning that it carries forward depend on the validity of the rainbow image. Without the rainbow we would have something radically different from what Lawrence in fact has achieved, and this novel, which occupies the central position between *Sons and Lovers* and *Women in Love,* could not be—as I think it is—a higher achievement than its predecessor or successor.[1]

The major clue to the success of Lawrence's conclusion to *The*

---

[1] F. R. Leavis thinks otherwise. See *D. H. Lawrence: Novelist* (New York, 1956), p. 111.

Rainbow[2] lies in the criticism of the failure in *Sons and Lovers* . . .

Tested against the criteria of character-growth and significant struggle *Sons and Lovers* fails as a *Bildungsroman* where, traditionally, the hero meets the experiences of life by trial and error, by suffering and failure, and at the end is rewarded for his trials by faith and for his errors by knowledge. Whatever one says about the ending of *Sons and Lovers*, one fact is abundantly clear: Paul Morel's experience of the world has made him neither wise nor foolish but rather helpless. And the sudden shift in direction at the close betrays confusion and a poor sense of timing more than impatience: Lawrence had not yet solved what his hero was to do with his experience—if, indeed, it had been experience at all. Yet, in spite of the faltering at the end, Lawrence intuitively, I think, meant to have the sudden turn, just as later he fully intended to give us (and his heroine)—at the right moment—the image of the rainbow. Lawrence insisted with vigour that the novel had form: 'I tell you it has got form—*form*,'[3] he wrote to Garnett, and one supposes he meant chiefly that *Sons and Lovers* was well constructed (which it was), unaware perhaps that it lacked the sort of form that goes beyond construction to attain a dimension of psychological truth. When Lawrence wrote to Garnett about his intentions in *The Rainbow* he spoke of gaining that dimension in what he considered a new way altogether: 'I don't care about physiology of matter—but somehow—that which is physic—non-human, in

---

[2] Two strong objections to the conclusion of *The Rainbow* are raised by Leavis and Graham Hough. Although he admires *The Rainbow* and thinks it a unique book, Leavis feels that there are 'signs of too great a tentativeness in the development and organization of the later part; signs of a growing sense in the writer of an absence of any conclusion in view' (p. 172). He also feels that the rainbow vision is 'a note wholly unprepared and unsupported, defying the preceding pages' (p. 170). This position is supported by Graham Hough, *The Dark Sun, A Study of D. H. Lawrence* (London, 1956), p. 71: 'the book can have no proper ending . . . we can only feel that . . . the rainbow vision is quite insufficiently based, nothing in the book up to now has led up to it.' Arnold Kettle, in an otherwise useful essay, concludes with a strong social indictment of Lawrence and of the rainbow image: 'the final image of the rainbow, upon which almost everything, artistically, must depend,[2] is not a triumphant image resolving in itself the half-clarified contradictions brought into play throughout the book, but a misty, vague and unrealized vision which gives us no more than the general sense that Lawrence is, after all, on the side of life' (*An Introduction to the English Novel*, London 1953, II, 131). The most recent attack on *The Rainbow* (though it is not a total condemnation) was published after the present essay was completed. S. L. Goldberg, in '*The Rainbow*: Fiddle-Bow and Sand', *Essays in Criticism*, XI (October 1961), finds, in general, that the ideology and the artistry of the novel are unresolved. He underscores the 'emotional falsity of the last few pages' (p. 427); finds the second half of the novel weaker than the first; accuses Lawrence of 'romantic assumptions . . . impatience and vagueness . . . in the last pages' (pp. 431–2); and sees the rainbow image as a culminating 'weakness that is obviously more than stylistic and is also more than local' (pp. 426–7).

[3] *Selected Literary Criticism*, p. 13.

humanity, is more interesting to me than the old-fashioned human element—which causes one to conceive a character in a certain moral scheme and make him consistent.... You mustn't look in my novel for the old stable *ego* of the character. There is another *ego*.'[4]

Since Ursula is after all the heroine of *The Rainbow*, it is to her that we look for the book's texture. And—Lawrence to the contrary—Ursula is really more human than non-human, more a stable ego than a plastic psyche; old-fashioned she may not be, but she is both consistent (to her inner self) and inescapably committed to a 'moral scheme', if such commitment implies an honest confrontation of life in the search for truth. The consistent—and human—character within a moral scheme: that has always been the traditional framework of the *Bildungsroman*; and a careful reading of *The Rainbow* reveals not a less traditional novel than *Sons and Lovers* (as Lawrence thought) but a traditional novel which has made its own space in the continuum. What Lawrence could not solve in *Sons and Lovers* he did solve in *The Rainbow*. This is not to imply that the novel is entirely conventional, or that Ursula is wholly a stable ego, for the timely ritual scenes —the moon episodes, the cathedral tableau—do attempt to convey some sense of a plastic psyche being moulded beneath the character's secondary ego.

In rejecting the Proustian and Joycean techniques of projecting their characters' inner life, Lawrence substituted a real persona whose psyche would operate as a kind of anti-self. In that way the hero's journey through experience would become a sort of dialogue of self and soul, a dialectic between the character's objective experience and his subjective assimilation of it. This provided the novel with a realism without depriving it of the psychological subtleties that Joyce or Virginia Woolf achieved by different routes. But the ritual scenes occur less frequently in *The Rainbow* than they do in *Women in Love* where, it is fair to say, they form the very choreography of the novel, holding it in place with delicately interlaced continuity. On close inspection, the letter to Garnett more accurately applies to *Women in Love*. In *The Rainbow*, the ritual scenes arrest, at crucial points, the more traditional narrative of the hero's pilgrimage toward knowledge; but, from each of these climatic pictorial dramas, Lawrence moves back to the central motion of his story. So that in the end, the stable ego is somehow made to accommodate the plastic ego. Ursula remains a fully realized character, whose inner life has been almost completely appropriated by her outer. Pared to the bone of her Being as she is at the end, we think of her, as we leave the novel, as character rather than psyche. And we feel, as we do not always feel in Lawrence, that the author has cared for that character: it makes for a unique accomplishment of integration—perhaps correlation is a better term—between

[4] Ibid., pp. 17–18.

the intentional direction of the artist and the demands that his character seems to have made against them. It is a triumph which Lawrence failed to repeat, not because his powers declined but because by the time he wrote *Women in Love,* he had truly achieved another—and radically different—dimension, from which there was no turning back.

II

The Rainbow, as we know, was scheduled at one point in its writing —when *Women in Love* was not yet conceived of as a separate novel —to be entitled *The Wedding Ring*; that title proved to be unsuitable for both novels. Lawrence probably rejected the title for *The Rainbow,* in spite of its apparent aptness to the marriage theme traced through several generations, because the ring image, wrongly conceived, might contradict an essential element of meaning in the novel. For it is Ursula's express triumph over her experience to break through all circles, all encircling hindrances, and among them, particularly, the circle of the wedding ring. Even in *Women in Love* she still rejects the ring, flinging Birkin's gift of three rings into the mud; and she can only accept the rings when they are joined by the flower, which she brings to her reconciliation with Birkin as a symbol of continuing growth. It is growth, indeed, that *The Rainbow* is centrally occupied with : two long chapters in the novel are headed 'The Widening Circle', and both circles—the first leading from childhood to adolescence, the second from adolescence to adulthood—as they increase in circumference increase in the threat of enclosing and arresting Ursula's growth. Paradoxically, the widening circles cannot keep pace with the widening of Ursula's aspiring soul, and the larger her world becomes, the more acute is her realization of its limitations. Growth is Ursula's emblem: at times, as in the moon scene, it is a frightening, inhuman vitality, saved only by the humanness of character which Lawrence succeeds in building into her. Experience may be a teacher, but to Ursula it is more than that—it is the very motive of life, something she hunts out as an end in itself (though the rainbow is at the end of it) until, in *Women in Love,* Lawrence, through Birkin, teaches her its limitations. At the beginning of *Women in Love,* when Gudrun and Ursula talk discursively about marriage, Gudrun suggests that the experience of wifehood may, after all, be a necessary treasure in one's life. But Ursula is sceptical that marriage *is* an experience: 'More likely', she says, 'to be the end of experience.'

This voracious appetite for experience is not unique with Ursula: her mother, Anna, possessed it in its barest state, and her grandmother, Lydia, had merely disguised it under her aristocratic pretensions, her 'foreignness'. One aim in tracing the three generations of women is to demonstrate the progressive shades of meaning in their appetites for experience: in Lydia it is partially subdued by convention, only to stir underneath as melancholia and frustration; in Anna it is wild and undirected and self-consuming. Only in Ursula does this appetite become truly attached to a conscious being, become, ultimately, directed and *civilized*. Therefore, the striving—and the failure of achievement —of the earlier generations prepares us for the vital centre of the novel: the education of Ursula, through whom the preceding, and partial, impulses are carried to successful completion.

In the opening pages of *The Rainbow* we are told that the women looked to the 'spoken world beyond', to the Word within the World. Facing outward, just as the men face inward, the women seek to fulfil their 'range of motion' by searching for 'knowledge', 'education', and 'experience'. Only Ursula finds all three—and finds them wanting. Anna is a primitive version of Ursula, and her experiences so often resemble Ursula's that Lawrence at times seems almost to be straining the point. But the differences are more significant than the similarities, for Anna remains unconscious, to the end, of the full meaning of her experiences. Her main defence against the encircling world and roofed-in arch of the church is multiplication of self: by producing scores of children she erects a kind of shield around herself. But children remain at best unwilling ambassadors and cannot negotiate for her. Ursula realizes this almost from the start as she chooses the opposite way: not padding the self protectively but stripping it to the core.

In the harvest scene between Will and Anna, the latter reveals the doomed nature of her relationship with life which consists in trying to achieve the impossible simultaneity of isolation and relatedness, the repulsion of being within the ring (of marriage) and the passionate necessity to possess its very centre. There is no Birkin here who can explain the complex 'star equilibrium' in which a man and a woman find separateness in union. Anna is torn between what she fears most and craves most, and it is this scene which clearly presages her future. It is a ritual, very Laurentian with its moon and mood of incantation. Anna is always first in returning her harvest to the stooks. As Will comes with his bundle Anna leaves: it is a 'rhythm' in which she 'drift[s] and ebb[s] like a wave'. But the rhythm that keeps them together keeps them apart: 'As he came, she drew away, as he drew away, she came. Were they never to meet?' Always there remains the 'space between them' until at last they meet and make love—until, that is, Anna, with her Brangwen passion, subdues her opposing Will.

Now the point of this scene is, in part, to convey Anna's violation of the rhythm that had kept her apart from intimacy; or, to put it differently, to show how she chooses one way, though committed to another. The intimacy is all too temporary, severed during the fortnight of honeymoon. And the 'space between them' is never finally breached. Anna's pursuit of experience is therefore always blinded by the insistent demands of an inner resistance to accept experience, to go through with it to the end in order to test its validity. Ursula commits herself to experience in the full knowledge of risk and is willing to taste—again and again—the ashen fruits of the experiences that fail her—religion, education, knowledge, passion. Anna's incomplete and arrested tilt with experience rewards her with only an incomplete and arrested vision of the rainbow, and Lawrence could not be clearer about his meaning:

> Dawn and sunset were the feet of the rainbow that spanned the day, and she saw the hope, the promise. Why should she travel any further?
> Yet she always asked the question. As the sun went down . . . she faced the blazing close of the affair, in which she *had not played her fullest part,* and she made her demand still: 'What are you doing, making this big shining commotion?'
> . . . With satisfaction *she relinquished the adventure to the unknown.*
> . . . If she were not the wayfarer to the unknown, if she were arrived now, settled in her builded houses, a rich woman, still her doors opened under the arch of the rainbow, her threshold reflected the passing of the sun and moon, the great travellers, her house was full of the echo of journeying. [Italics mine]

Were Anna content with the 'echo of journeying' as a fit substitute for the journey itself, her attainment of family, house, and children would be well enough for creative life. But she is not content. And since she has no way of working out her discontent other than yearning for that in which she is unwilling, always, to play her full part—the experience of life measured to its ends—she is left with a finite vision after all, a rainbow whose two ends bind her to the rising and setting sun, to the limited existence of an everyday world.

It is a mistake Ursula does not make because she has the courage to face the annihilating, but paradoxically freedom-giving moment of having journeyed fully committed to the end of experience. In the central Cathedral scene, Anna 'claimed the right to freedom above her, higher than the roof. She had always a sense of being roofed in'; yet her claim is undercut by her incapacity to approach anything beyond the roof. She turns immediately to the gargoyles which she reduces, defensively, to human shapes, an act of reassurance, not of faith. Ursula's struggle for the beyond is differently shaped. To each new experience she brings the whole of herself. Her encounter with religion is total: she even plays out, against her intuition, the practical results of offering the other cheek, and only rejects the act after her cheeks burn with the slap of her sister's hand. Failing in religious faith she puts next her faith in love, though she enacts it, at first, amidst the ruins of her old faith, in the interior of the church which, with its fallen stones, its ruined plaster, its scaffolding, is all too symbolically under constant repair.

Always, with Ursula, there is yearning followed by enactment: she

never retreats, she always chooses. Three quarters through the novel
we find her amidst an emblematic landscape, which aptly projects
her state of being constantly on the verge of setting foot into another
world, of widening her circle:

> The blue way of the canal wound softly between the autumn hedges,
> on towards the greenness of a small hill. On the left was the whole
> black agitation of colliery and railway and the town which rose on its
> hill, the church tower topping all. The round white dot of the clock
> of the tower was distinct in the evening light.
> That way, Ursula felt, was the way to London, through the grim,
> alluring seethe of the town. On the other hand was the evening,
> mellow over the green watermeadows. . . .
> Ursula and Anton Skrebensky walked along the ridge of the canal
> between. . . . The glow of evening and the wheeling of the solitary
> pee-wit and the faint cry of the birds came to meet the shuffling noise
> of the pits, the dark, fuming stress of the town opposite, and they
> two walked the blue strip of water-way, the ribbon of sky between.

The canal divides the two shores which together form the whole of
Ursula's potential world and, incidently, the whole of the world which
she experiences in the novel. On the right lie the fields of her birth,
the fecund earth on which she and Skrebensky first consummate their
love; on the left lie the colliery, the town, the church, and London,
each of which is once tested and discarded. She rejects the fecund
earth when she renounces the blood-prescient nature of Anthony for
the sake of the journey onwards: 'But she was a traveller, she was a
traveller on the face of the earth, and he was an isolated creature living
in the fulfilment of his own senses.' The refusal of the church we
have already pointed to; with Winifred Inger, Ursula pushes away the
colliery of her uncle Tom—'impure abstraction, the mechanisms of
matter'—and London as well, the London of Miss Inger, sophisticated perversion. And the town, where Ursula is so brutally initiated
into the man's world, is gladly forsaken too: 'The stupid, artificial,
exaggerated town. . . . What is it?—nothing, just nothing.' She will
have to walk through the town, not towards it, like Paul Morel, and the
transcendence can only occur vertically toward a vision, since on the
horizontal plane—where Anna was always condemned to move—the
landscape of the world is, at the end of the novel, fully exhausted of
possibilities.

   To say that Ursula searches for selfhood is descriptive but not very
profoundly interpretive, for that fact is of lesser importance by far
than the manner of her search. I have already said that the growth of
Ursula's world coincides with the diminishing possibilities of her functioning creatively within it. From that point of view the novel is
largely negative, consisting of a number of refusals and rejections without any corresponding affirmations. But the search for self, in the

fitting image of husk and kernel at the end of the book, is a process of stripping away all layers that disguise and protect self from the truth of self (it resembles Lear's stripping process). So while the circle of the world widens, the circle of the self narrows in inverse proportion: the larger the one, the smaller—and the nearer to the core—the other. Ursula's annihilation of Skrebensky under the moon is no mere repetition of Anna's subjugation of Will under the same moon: it is, indeed, a far more violent and total act, but one with more results as well, and more motive. Ursula has the ability—which Anna lacked—to convert experience into knowledge: she masters the economics of experiencing to perfection. What she discovers is Skrebensky's lack of self and through it she is illumined on the nature of self—her own and in the abstract. She triumphs—not as Anna had, in order to subdue Will, but to create a self of her own. There under the moon she is awakened for the first time to the awful power of self—and its dangers; and it frightens her, enough to prevent her from severing her relationship with Skrebensky. It is true that her lust motivates her to 'tear him and make him into nothing', but that impulse itself spells out the nature of a ceaselessly moving self. After she destroys Skrebensky, her soul is, understandably enough, 'empty and finished': destruction has not come without its price. When he leaves she feels that emptiness even more acutely. Although she has seen the power of self she has not gained control of it by far, 'since she *had* no self'. Only after turning with shame and hatred on Winifred Inger and uncle Tom does she get any closer to it, and that double rejection makes way for her final struggles.

The last episodes with Skrebensky have puzzled a good many readers and some, like Hough, have suggested that Lawrence himself was not clear on the subject. Yet if Lawrence was not, Ursula was, for she predicts the failure of her resumed affair before she ever embarks on it: 'Passion is only part of love. And it seems so much because it can't last. That is why passion is never happy.' Yet, in the tradition of the hero undergoing the education of life, knowledge—of a kind—often precedes the experience that will confirm it. The true hero must always experience before he can truly know: he never substitutes intuitional wisdom for the living through itself. Often, as with Ursula, this is a conscious sacrifice at the altar of life's suffering, and it is consciousness, as I have said, that distinguishes Ursula as the kind of hero she is. 'Ursula suffered bitterly at the hands of life': and that is proper for the hero whom life educates in its bitter school. But consciousness makes such suffering even more intense and makes it so precisely because it injects and maintains some ideal toward which all action gravitates with certainty and direction. When she and Anthony face a beautiful sunset, it is Ursula's consciousness of its beauty that gives her the capacity for feeling pain—the pain that comes with recognizing the inevitable disparity between the achieved and the achievable. 'All this so beautiful, all this so lovely! He did not see it. He was one with it. But she saw it, and was one with it. Her seeing separated them infinitely.' Sight precedes perception; acknowledgment precedes knowledge.

It is this aspect of conscious perception in the pursuit of experience that I have earlier called civilized; but the cost of such awareness is very high and makes for the awful negation that burdens the whole novel. Ursula is hardly unaware of it: the pressure is always there, to seek out life, to encounter it in battle, to discard and to be defeated, and to move on again:

> She had the ash of disillusion gritting under her teeth. Would the next move turn out the same? Always the shining doorway ahead; and then, upon approach, always the shining doorway was a gate into another ugly yard. . . .
> No matter! Every hill-top was a little different, every valley was somehow new. . . .
> But what did it mean, Ursula Brangwen? She did not know what she was. Only she was full of rejection, of refusal. Always, always she was spitting out of her mouth the ash and grit of disillusion. . . . She could only stiffen in rejection, in rejection. She seemed always negative in her action.

Such is her state as Lawrence moves into the final pages of his story, and to extricate Ursula from her negation, to provide her with an earned vision at the close was, as is apparent, no easy task. At this point Ursula begins to perceive, dimly, a world outside experience, a world outside the 'circle lighted by a lamp', a world dark and mysterious where 'she saw the eyes of the wild beast gleaming'. Towards that world she must move, out of the circle of the lighted lamp, from the illumination of familiarity into the shadows of the unknown, truly the unknown. This constitutes the search beyond the finite self, the personal self.

One day, watching the sea roll in, she comes to know that through the self-consciousness of seeking life one is heir to the shocks of recognition which reveal what one has *not* attained, an exercise of the imagination which presupposes fulfilment of things the other side of the present. Touched by the beauty of the rhythmically moving sea—as she was by the sunset—she laughs and weeps from a single impulse. Then she follows 'a big wave running unnoticed, to burst in a shock of foam against a rock . . . leaving the rock emerged black and teeming'. Her wish for the fate of the wave is symbolic: 'Oh, and if, when the wave burst into whiteness, it were only set free!' If, that is, the wave, making its climatic collision with the rock of the opposing world, could only be liberated from its flux of experience, prevented somehow from falling into the sea again, only to become water for another wave. If only Ursula could fly the flux of her experience and bear away her trophy, the fruits of experience, to the safety of some timeless region that would not condemn her to this ceaseless repetition of battle with life. The image of the liberated wave resembles the circle lighted by a lamp, and both resemble the encircling horde of stallions at the end.

Ursula's final experience with the lighted circle of the world is her futile passion with Skrebensky, and it is preceded by the botany class-room scene in which Ursula makes her penultimate leap. She sees the speck under her microscope moving and it appears vitally alive, but Ursula questions its beingness, its teleology, if it has one: 'She only knew that it was not limited mechanical energy, nor mere purpose of self-preservation and self-assertion. It was a consummation, a being infinite.' By being a fully realized self, one could in fact fly the circle into a 'oneness with the infinite': 'To be oneself was a supreme, gleaming triumph of infinity.' To capture the wave out of the sea was to catapult it into the infinite reaches, where it might be preserved with wholeness. Such an insight followed by yet another disillusion-ment is not meaningless. The affair with Skrebensky, aside from pro-viding proof of what she has perceived, serves also to clarify the con-tours of the circle which Ursula must flee. Already as a school teacher she had felt increasingly the 'prison . . . round her'; and the sense of wishing to break out of the enclosing and binding circles becomes sharply defined in the penultimate chapter in which, on two occasions, the final rainbow image is clearly prefigured. 'This inner circle of light in which she lived and moved' has become too much to bear; and finally she would 'not love Skrebensky in a house any more'. She must go to the downs, into the open spaces, where in the darkness of night she experiences the final 'bitterness of ecstasy'. They await the dawn: 'She watched a pale rim on the sky. . . . The darkness became bluer. . . . The light grew stronger, gushing up against the dark . . . night. The light grew stronger, whiter, then over it hovered a flush of rose. A flush of rose, and then yellow . . . poising momentarily over the fountain on the sky's rim.' Here the spectrum of colours certainly sug-gests the rainbow—the rose burns, then turns to red; 'great waves of yellow' are flung over the sky, 'scattering its spray over the darkness, which became bluer and bluer . . . till soon it would itself be a radiance'. And finally the sun breaks through, 'too powerful to look at'. Some pages earlier appeared another image, also suggestive of the rainbow, and again Ursula and her lover were in the open: 'And in the roaring circle under the tree . . . they lay a moment looking at the twinkling lights on the darkness opposite, saw the sweeping brand of a train past the edge of their darkened field.' Such deliberate preparation hardly suggests haste and impatience when Lawrence came to the final pages of his novel.

III

That Ursula's journey through the widening circles of experience, and her ultimate flight beyond those circles into the arches of heaven, may be limited acts after all is a question Lawrence does not raise until *Women in Love*. There, in retrospect, Ursula sees at one point the possibility that even the exhaustion of experience may bring one only to the threshold of death. Socrates was right: the unexamined life was not worth living; but the modern novelist had to ask whether the examined life was worth living: 'She had travelled all her life along the line of fulfilment, and it was nearly concluded. She knew all she had to know, she had experienced all she had to experience, she was fulfilled in a kind of bitter ripeness, there remained only to fall from the tree into death.'

But in *The Rainbow* it is not the falling into death but the falling away from it which dominates as an image. In the scene with the stallions Ursula finally accomplishes her transcendence of the circles, precisely by letting herself drop from a tree. In doing so she fulfils the wish given us in an earlier image: 'She saw herself travelling round a circle, only an arc of which remained to complete. Then, she was in the open, like a bird tossed into mid-air, a bird that had learned in some measure to fly.' Repeatedly the horses come to ring her—'Like circles of lightning came the flash of hoofs'; 'They had gone by, brandishing themselves thunderously about her, enclosing her.' As the circle closes, every horizontal route of escape 'to the highroad and the ordered world of man' is cut off. There is only one way she can move —up: 'She might climb into the boughs of that oak tree, and so round and drop on the other side of the hedge.' So she proceeds; and her symbolic drop liberates her—as such drops often do in literature— into a consciousness of separateness done with temporal and spatial dimensions of world: 'time and the flux of change passed away from her, she lay as if unconscious ... like a stone ... unchanging ... whilst everything rolled by in transcience . . . [she was] sunk to the bottom of all change.' Now may the kernel shed the enclosing husk and 'take itself the bed of a new sky'; only the child remains: 'it bound her ... like a bond round her brain, tightened on her brain.' But when that bond is loosened she is ready for her rainbow—ready because free at last from the perpetuity of experience which had victimized her for so long. There is no taking the past away, for it had to be; only the full commitment to the circles of experience allows one to escape them. Ursula has escaped the fate of her father, who had gained 'knowledge and skill without vision'.

At the end of the novel there is no doubt that the reader has earned a vision of the rainbow, for he, unlike Ursula, has been subjected to the struggle of not one but three generations. But, if we look upon *The Rainbow* as a modern *Bildungsroman*, a trial and error warfare with experience, which allows finally a glimpse of an ideal that rises inevitably out of experience, then there can be little doubt that Ursula too has earned the right to her open, semi-circular rainbow, leaving her free like a bird 'that has learned in some measure to fly'.[5]

In none of the three major novels—*Sons and Lovers, The Rainbow, Women in Love*—does Lawrence resolve his ending as the logical, inevitable conclusion to a single ruling passion. Had he done so Paul Morel should have committed suicide; Ursula should have died of her heavy losses; and *Women in Love* should have been altogether an impossible book to write. Those who accuse Lawrence of a sleight of hand at the end of these novels fail to see the intuition and later the consciousness of his purpose, for he was quite aware that his conclusions were not the neat, conventional climaxes that satisfy a reader's expectations because they are coincident with his prophecies. Such endings he would have considered 'immoral':

> Because *no* emotion is supreme, or exclusively worth living for or dying for, he might have added. *All* emotions go to the achieving of a living relationship between a human being and the other human being or creature or thing he becomes purely related to.... If the novelist puts his thumb in the pan, for love, tenderness, sweetness, peace, then he commits an immoral act: he *prevents* the possibility of a pure relationship, a pure relatedness ... and he makes inevitable the horrible reaction, when he lets his thumb go, towards hate and brutality, cruelty and destruction.[6]

No one emotion carried to its end tells the whole truth, because it obstructs the basic complexity of the human psyche, its multifarious potential to act, to fulfil, at many levels, its inner needs in balance with the outer demands of the world. 'The business of art is to reveal the relation between man and his circumambient universe, at the living moment.' Lawrence goes on to call this 'living moment' a 'fourth dimension', 'a revelation of the perfected relation, at a certain moment, between a man' and his object. And that 'which exists in the non-dimensional space of pure relationship is deathless, lifeless, and eternal ... beyond life, and therefore beyond death.'[7] So precisely does Ursula exist at the conclusion of *The Rainbow*. Here Lawrence succeeded in capturing the 'momentaneous' (it is a favourite word) in the midst of timelessness: this is the essential meaning of the rainbow. Ursula's 'living moment' is therefore beyond life or death, in the fourth dimension where neither hope nor despair has any business.

In its demand that the hero experience—indeed, that he seek out

---

[5] Like Lear, Ursula is freed from the 'wheel of fire', 'the rack of this tough world'; Lawrence felt that 'Lear was essentially happy, even in his greatest misery' (*Selected Literary Criticism*, p. 123), just as Yeats considered Lear 'gay' in 'Lapis Lazuli'. Lawrence might have entitled his penultimate chapter 'The Ecstasy of Bitterness', instead of 'The Bitterness of Ecstasy' ...

[6] 'The Morality of the Novel', *Selected Literary Criticism*, p. 110.

[7] *Ibid.*, pp. 108–9.

experience—and suffer for it, *The Rainbow* remains an entirely conventional *Bildungsroman*, a type of novel naturally suited to a man of Lawrence's passionate pedagogic temperament. But in rejecting, at the end, both the hero who is a helpless victim of experience and the hero whom experience transforms into a malcontent, Lawrence achieved a new dimension for the novel of education in the twentieth century: the hero has been '*emotionally* educated which is rare as a phoenix'.[8] Here lies the true originality of form in *The Rainbow*: at the end of experience the hero has gained the privilege of release from it; and the *Lehrjahre*—post-apprenticeship learning—really lie ahead in the *Wanderjahre*, in the inconclusiveness of *Women in Love*, where experience is not tested against the world but against one's self. The end of experience, in the modern world, is only the beginning of selfhood. Life is no longer just a school nor experience a mere teacher: both have become antagonists to conquer in exchange for freedom. It it is a fair war since Lawrence never refuses to exact the price of suffering. The 'human moral', having fully tested the 'social moral', is at liberty to discriminate. Such a view of experience has influenced a writer like Hemingway (one of the few modern novelists Lawrence admired), whose heroes—despite their hunger for experience—wish finally to become educated 'emotionally' and thereby be liberated from the compulsive tests of experience, Hemingway going Lawrence one better by suggesting a 'fifth dimension' in which this might be achieved. Certainly the ending of *The Old Man and the Sea* owes something in spirit to that of *The Rainbow*: after the worst that experience can inflict, the old man comes home to dream of the lions on the beach.

'While a man remains a man, a true human individual,' Lawrence insisted, 'there is at the core of him a certain innocence or naïveté. ... This does not mean that the human being is nothing but naive or innocent. He is Mr Worldly Wiseman also to his own degree. But in his essential core he is naive.'[9] Here surely is an account of Ursula as we find her at the end of the novel: worldly-wise but purged, and at the core innocent. For Goethe the end of experience was also the end of innocence, for in his world the hero's path was still clearly marked so that, in proportion as the hero grew wise, he would choose the right way: the flux of experience gave way to the steadiness of wisdom. For Lawrence—as for others, of course,—the modern world offered no such clear topography ... Ursula reaches no 'happy goal' at the end of her experience in *The Rainbow*, and the novelist, like his heroine, had to begin again, from a different perspective, where Goethe could contentedly end.[10]

[8] *Ibid.*, p. 118.
[9] *Ibid.*, p. 120.
[10] ... One has finally to meet the objection—implicit in most critiques of the rainbow symbol—that, on the literal level, the rainbow is a temporary, trans-

PMLA, LXXVIII (March, 1963).

itory image: rainbows give way to different weather. But Lawrence was fully aware of this: *The Rainbow* gave way to a different novel. The very transitoriness of the rainbow makes it a proper and significant symbol for, at the end of the novel, Ursula is meant to be projected into that fourth dimension, suspended between an end and a beginning. It is a position of respite from which she will later re-enter the world; though neither she nor the world will be the same.

F. H. LANGMAN

Women in Love

I

Women in Love is widely accepted, now, as what F. R. Leavis showed it to be: the major work of a major novelist. And its more recent critics have largely agreed not only on its merits but also on its faults. In their view Lawrence failed to resolve problems he believed that he was resolving, or at least set out to resolve, and following from this supposed failure of thought they see a failure of structure. Dr Leavis's statement of the case remains the clearest: 'The diagnosis represented by Gerald and Gudrun is convincing—terribly so; but Birkin and Ursula as a norm, contemplated in the situation they are left in at the close of the book, leave us wondering (and, it must in fairness be added, leave Lawrence wondering too). That is, if a certain symmetry of negative and positive was aimed at in *Women in Love*, Lawrence has been defeated by the difficulty of life: he hasn't solved the problems of civilization that he analyses.'[1]

This criticism, which has been repeated[2] by critics as different as Eliseo Vivas and W. W. Robson, rests on some questionable assumptions. One is that Lawrence's intention in the novel can be known apart from, and used as a measure of, his achievement. Another is that the novel is constructed on a simple pattern of contrast—a symmetry of negative and positive—between the complete failure of one love affair and the assured success of the other. A third is that an adequate criticism of any novel can approach it as an analysis of the problems of civilization, to be judged by whether, on a simple practical level, it offers a viable solution. To question these assumptions is not, of course, to accept the absolute divorce of poetry from prophecy, art from message or moral, that Vivas for one (although his practice is inconsistent) demands in theory.

Lawrence's intentions in writing *Women in Love*, whatever they may have been, are beside the point. The tale, if we trust it, simply does not present the marriage of Birkin and Ursula as ideal in itself

---

[1] F. R. Leavis, *D. H. Lawrence: Novelist* (London 1955), p. 28.

[2] Eliseo Vivas, *D. H. Lawrence: the Failure and the Triumph of Art* (London 1961), pp. 266–7; W. W. Robson, 'D. H. Lawrence and *Women in Love*', *The Modern Age* (Harmondsworth, 1961), p. 299. It is curious that both of these writers criticize Dr Leavis as if without qualification he accepted the marriage of Birkin and Ursula as successfully setting up a norm.

or as an adequate solution to the problems presented. On the contrary, an important thesis of the novel is that no fully satisfying personal relationship is possible to people placed, like Birkin and Ursula, in a social and religious vacuum. Lawrence's treatment of their marriage is firmer and less 'positive', shows a keener awareness of life's difficulties, than any attempt to set up a norm could offer. It follows from this that the structure of the novel must be less symmetrical and more complex than has been supposed. Birkin and Gerald, in particular, are not so diagrammatically opposed. Their destinies do not represent the assured positive solution and a disastrous deviation from it, but something far less definite: a contrast of attitudes, hope against despair, struggle against surrender.

The subtle structure the novel actually evolves, in not making just that false simplification its critics have thought to see in it, may be brought out better by attention to the form rather than the ostensible meaning of the two love-stories. The Gerald-Gudrun story is closed, it forms a complete action in the Aristotelian sense. The Birkin-Ursula story is open. It has a beginning and a development, but no end either displayed or implied. The future of this story is not predetermined, and the agents move out of the last pages into the freedom of continued, unpredictable, endeavour. Looking back over the novel from the clear and conscious inconclusiveness of the final paragraph, we can see that this freedom, this making of choices in a continual process of self-commitment, has characterized this couple at every stage of the story. Gerald on the other hand is fated. His doom is fixed from the start, and he abandons himself to the remorseless forces which carry him to it. These forces act as much from within himself as from without, but still he cannot be said to choose his direction. He acquiesces in it, lets himself go; and, paradoxically, this passivity towards his fate, towards the forces of destruction within himself, takes the form of an exertion of the will ... Gudrun is caught up in the same processes, and although she does not literally die her future course too has, by the end of the novel, been rigidly and terrifyingly predetermined.

This contrast of form between the two stories leads to a more satisfying evaluation of the novel than the usual way of judging it on what it offers of social diagnosis and therapy. I do not mean that *Women in Love* is not concerned—and very directly—with social analysis. Modern society is its subject, but its approach is more exploratory than prescriptive. The closed story defines its own moral, but within the context of a larger complexity. Gerald's death is only an episode in Birkin's life. The open story is the more inclusive of the two, and to recognize this is to see the vital role in the novel of speculation, choice, quest, and incompletion.

II

Lawrence's earlier critics made it necessary for Dr Leavis to stress his rootedness in the English tradition, but more recent commentators[3] are surely right, too, in comparing Lawrence with such European writers as Nietzsche and Dostoevsky. In saying this, I do not mean to support anything as limited (and in my view, mistaken) as the attempt by Dr Panichas to trace an influence through specific parallels between *Crime and Punishment* and *Women in Love*. I wish, rather, to suggest Lawrence's scope and status. His deepest preoccupations were with problems which took their most acute forms, historically, in Europe, and received their most intense artistic expression not in English. It is very telling that the last movement of *Women in Love* should begin with a journey far into Europe to arrive at the figure, gone so much further down the 'tunnel of darkness' than any of the English characters, of the polyglot Loerke. *Women in Love* places Lawrence in the line of European writers who, from Dostoevsky on, have made the novel the medium of at once the most deeply felt social awareness and the most urgent philosophical speculation. In this line—surely the main line of the modern novel—the important writers in England have been Lawrence and Conrad. Conrad's place in the line seems clear. It may not be as readily granted of Lawrence, but the essential similarity is there, as I shall try to show. . . .

. . . At any rate, I suggest that *Women in Love* gets much of its significance from the same scepticism, the same double sense of things, as we find in Conrad. It affirms the necessity of the social bond and explores the values out of which the bond can be renewed, but it acknowledges with bleak honesty that it can go only some part of the way towards discovering values that will suffice, and it denies the source of the old values. For the primary fact of *Women in Love* is that none of its characters can continue to believe in God. Its essential drama, for all its concern with the forms and pressures of English society, is on the familiar theme of modern European novels: the search for the vanished God or for surrogates of divinity. Some of its characters, like Hermione, throne the human understanding paramount and make of that their God. Some, like Gerald, seek escape in distraction—art, or sex, or social welfare, or work. Ursula and Birkin look openly on their despair and seek beyond it.

This is what drives Gerald to his death. His self-distractions fail one by one, power, work, love. Confronting at last his own unmitigated emptiness, he flies from it into extinction, the oblivion of the snow. In his last moments he finds, half-buried in the snow, a crucifix. But this cannot help him now. He sheers away, and his will to live snaps. It is not that he accepts the conditions of life, comes to terms with death. For him, to die is to be murdered. 'Some-

---

[3] See Eugene Goodheart, *The Utopian Vision of D. H. Lawrence* (Chicago 1963) and George A. Panichas, *Adventure in Consciousness: The Meaning of D. H. Lawrence's Religious Quest* (The Hague, 1964).

body was going to murder him.' His last conscious thought is made to be a helpless invocation of the disavowed saviour: 'Lord Jesus, was it then bound to be—Lord Jesus!' This, with its note of awe, its atavistic appeal, is immensely powerful, but its power is in irony. What it reflects is Gerald's failure to find any sustaining belief: it is a surrender, not a prayer and not an affirmation.

The same quest uproots Birkin and Ursula, and sets them wandering. Birkin longs for a new, more congenial community, but for this the prerequisite is a new faith. He seeks a faith to breathe life back into social relationships. The society he knows stultifies him, not because of its external ugliness but because it lacks meaning. It has failed to create new values adequate to its experience. He feels 'imprisoned within a limited false set of concepts'. His exile, a deliberate cutting free from the old social ties, may be necessary to a new beginning but does not, of itself cannot, bring what he seeks. The novel ends, as it begins, not with bold answers but with painful questioning.

Despite the obvious—and on Lawrence's part conscious—differences between them, this particular conjoining of affirmation and scepticism indicates the measure of Lawrence's affinity with Conrad. Of the two, Lawrence is really the more intransigent. 'I can't forgive Conrad for being so sad and for giving in'—it is the spirit of that (whatever its unfairness to Conrad) which makes Lawrence's scepticism so firm, so radical: the power of negation in *Women in Love*, the continued undermining of hopeful attitudes, is itself a form of not giving in. Yet it is every bit as desolate and disconcerting a novel as, say, *Nostromo* or *Under Western Eyes*.

To define the affinity more sharply, to search for specific parallels between one novel and another, has its obvious dangers, but there are resemblances between the central metaphors of *Women in Love* and *Lord Jim* which provide some confirmation of my argument, and carry it further. I hope the comparison will not seem forced: it is offered as suggestive rather than conclusive. In *Lord Jim*, then, the hero deserts an apparently sinking ship, abandoning the unsuspecting passengers to their fate. . . .

. . . Lord Jim leaps into the abyss of freedom in a moment of panic and weakness. Lawrence's characters—the difference is significant—are borne down half-willingly in a lingering letting-go. But what they find is the same. They are set free for any excess, any abomination. So Gudrun and Gerald recognize in each other 'the subterranean desire to let go, to fling away everything, and lapse into a sheer unrestraint, brutal and licentious'.

These images running through the novel suggest, as in Conrad, that as with moral laws so the purposes of individuals take their form from social life. When society fails, a man alone, though in touch with immensity, can find neither goal nor guide. This is made explicit not by Gerald but by Birkin, the novel's 'positive' spokesman:

'The old ideals are dead as nails—nothing there.
It seems to me there remains only this perfect union with a woman —sort of ultimate marriage—and there isn't anything else.'
'And you mean if there isn't the woman, there's nothing?' said Gerald.
'Pretty well that—seeing there's no God.'

Faced with the death of the old ideals, how thin, how minimal, Birkin's positive is: how close to sheer negation. All that he has is a tentative willingness, insistent rather than confident, to let life make a claim on him. So he says 'I want to love'. He wants, that is in the lack of any clear belief, to be committed by his emotions (as, later, Gerald's instinct leads him to Gudrun). Nor, even in this, is Birkin clear and unwavering. In Chapter VIII, after Hermione has attempted to kill him, he enacts half-consciously a kind of ritual of purification in a wild thicket. He takes off his clothes, takes off the insignia as it were of his membership in society, and consummates what he thinks of as his marriage to the natural world. When he comes to himself he thinks of his wish for love as a mistake, he feels weary of the old ethic that bade a human being adhere to humanity. Birkin's religion—despite his explicit disavowal he is haunted by a vague, vestigial sense of the Godhead, what he calls the 'creative utterances', the 'unseen hosts'— does not alleviate the novel's despair. It suggests no answer, or only the saddest of all possible answers, to the problems of civilization:

Let mankind pass away—time it did. . . . Humanity doesn't embody the utterance of the incomprehensible any more.

This is ultimate despair. This is, expressed here in direct words and expressed by Birkin, what Gerald's death in the snow means. And against this despair, at the conceptual level, at the level of argument, Birkin has nothing positive to offer.

But in Birkin the mood is unable to sustain itself. He cannot drive the image of the moon—Cybele, Syria Dea, the universal urge to love and creation—from the surface of the pond, nor permanently shatter it. Deny it though he may, the old ethic in him is ineradicable. Ursula forces from him the admission that, though he calls it his disease, he does love humanity and cannot forsake it. Nor is he able to resist the old human need to interpret, after all, the utterances of the incomprehensible: 'it is the law of creation. One is committed. One must commit oneself to a conjunction with the other.' So he looks to marriage to provide his own life with a centre. From here, he comes to see marriage as the basis of a community, to think of society as held together not by work or any unifying idea but by love, by the bonds of feeling between man and woman and man and man. Marriage is the first step, friendship is the second. As soon as his relationship with Ursula is securely established, his thoughts turn to the inclusion in their 'separate world' of a few other people, to the formation of a new community 'where one meets a few people who have gone through enough, and can take things for granted. . . . There is somewhere—there are one or two people'.

There is no need to dilate on the deficiencies of this, and to contend against it as if it were put forward without qualification as a norm would miss the point. The very wistfulness of the utterance contains an implicit criticism of it, and in the outcome Birkin's wish is utterly thwarted. Whether his ideas are true or false, possible or impossible, remains in question to the very last words of the novel. The end of the novel brings back, confirms, the unbearable sadness of Birkin's vision in the wild valley before the experiment of marriage began.

Either the heart would break, or cease to care. Best cease to care. Whatever the mystery which had brought forth man and the universe, it is a non-human mystery, it has its own great ends, man is not the criterion.

The most painful question in the whole novel, a question that precisely places the limited value of the experiment in marriage, is Ursula's: 'Why aren't I enough?' . . .

Essays in Criticism, Vol. XVII, No. 2, April 1967, pp. 183–93.

CURTIS ATKINSON

Was There Fact in D. H. Lawrence's *Kangaroo*?

In his article 'D. H. Lawrence's *Kangaroo*: Fantasy, Fact or Fiction?' (*Meanjin Quarterly*, June, 1965), John Alexander seems to have missed an incident, or series of incidents, which may throw light on the politics of the novel. These took place in Sydney a year before Lawrence wrote *Kangaroo* at Thirroul, about thirty miles south of Sydney.

On Sunday, May 1, 1921, a Labour meeting was held at the Sydney Town Hall under Trades Hall auspices. It purported to be a sort of memorial meeting to Percy Brookfield, a popular Labour figure, who had recently died. Some speakers introduced irrelevant abuse of returned soldiers. A counter-demonstration was organized in the Domain on the following Sunday amid great excitement. Newspaper editorials and correspondence kept the controversy alive. On Friday, May 6, a 'great patriotic demonstration' was held in the Town Hall, and the next day the *Sydney Morning Herald* published long reports. The climax of public clamour occurred on Sunday, May 8, when a crowd estimated at around 100,000 rioted in the Domain, broke up all meetings and stopped short of violence only because of the presence of a strong police squad.

The centre of the disturbance was the platform of the A.I.F. Returned Soldiers' Political League, at which I was a speaker. According to the *Sydney Morning Herald* (May 9, 1921), I described myself as 'a patriotic Englishman who denounced the encouragement of anti-British and anti-Australian sentiments.' The report went on to relate that C. H. Murphy, Labour M.L.A., was severely heckled and when the crowd surged round the lorry the police took him into protective custody and refused to allow the invaders to hold a meeting of their own. Elsewhere in the Domain a socialist and a communist meeting were broken up and portable platforms smashed.

I had noticed that about half the crowd was in uniform; the rest wore badges of the Returned Soldiers' League. State R.S.L. branches had sent contingents and had asked members to wear uniforms, and it was easy to see that many faces were inflamed; reports were current that as the groups formed up outside the Domain, liquor was passed around to boost emotions. I do not doubt the truth of these reports. The next day's *Herald* displayed across eight columns a picture of the immense crowd, with long descriptive reports.

Many people have guessed about the politics of *Kangaroo*. My 'guess' is that Lawrence had heard and/or read about the climate of opinion which existed not very long before his arrival in Australia. The events in Sydney I have briefly described were more than a nine-days' wonder; they left their mark on the politics of the period and on organizations like the R.S.L. for long afterwards. Flash-point was not so nearly reached again, but 'the accumulating forces of social violence' took years to simmer down.

Lawrence was known to be a tireless questioner on any subject which interested him. He was sufficiently interested in the political situation, as he glimpsed it, to write *Kangaroo*. It is regrettable that he was not more interested, so that he could have put more of the essential truth into the novel.

Meanjin Quarterly, September, 1965.

G. B. McK. HENRY

Carrying on:
Lady Chatterley's Lover

But in life, the curtain never comes down on the scene. There the dead bodies lie, and the inert ones, and somebody has to clear them away, somebody has to carry on. (*A Propos of Lady Chatterley's Lover.*)

Lawrence was right. How else can one explain the neglect and misunderstanding his last novel has suffered, the suspicion and nervous titters that the 'doctrine' it is too often supposed to be propaganda for has met, but as a general mistrust of sex? Even his admirers turn up their noses—'offences against taste' says Leavis; and in a recent excellent comprehensive study, *The Art of D. H. Lawrence* (C.U.P., 1966), Dr Keith Sagar's admirably rational and sensitive discussion breaks down into: 'The full accompaniment of Lawrence's prose cannot quite reconcile us to the persistent indulgence in copulation,' as he charges the novel with 'insistent, obsessive sexuality'. Lawrence is somewhat to blame for anticipating the reaction; he called it a 'phallic novel', so it's treated as a phallic novel (whatever that means) come what may. At least Graham Hough, while reluctant to admit the indispensability of the notorious explicitness, is sufficiently sympathetic to wonder whether 'the book is more successful as a novel . . . than as the sexual tract it is often taken to be'.

Of course Lawrence's insistence on the book's clean purpose is unfortunately not confined to the letters and *A Propos*; it appears in the novel as a recurrent corrective and self-justifying note—as in the famous passage relating the function of novels to the 'passional secret places of life'. In other words the didactic element is obvious and most of the faults of the novel can be attributed to it. They suggest that Lawrence's interest in people as individuals, human *beings,* had faded into an irritated dismissal of them as labelled types fully known long ago. The clumsy laxity of parts of the novel, that is, only indicates how peripheral those parts are. Lawrence had spent so much effort peeling off the layers of personality and social being ('the old stable ego' of fictional characters) to arrive at the essential 'carbon' of humanity, that in his later work he finds it very easy to generalize from his characters, to assume that their behaviour and ideas are *in fact representative* in the English class structure. Thus he suggests that Clifford's paralysis symbolizes 'the deeper emotional or passional paralysis of *most men of his sort and class today*' (*A Propos*, my italics); the generalization is wild enough to contain some truth. The effects, though, are unmistakable in the treatment of Clifford and his 'cronies' —the conversations are all too comfortably managed, Clifford's pronouncements tend to be used as typical examples of modern intellectual idiocy to be ridiculed, rather than as beliefs to be explored and tested:

> 'The universe shows us two aspects: on one side it is physically wasting, on the other it is spiritually ascending. ... It is thus slowly passing, with a slowness inconceivable in our measures of time, to new creative conditions, amid which the physical world, as we at present know it, will be represented by a ripple barely to be distinguished from nonentity.'

That is hardly a worthy object for Lawrence's or even Connie's satire. Elsewhere we seem invited to judge the book by the Kinsey report or something, as when Mellors asserts that 'most folks live their lives through' without knowing the delight of 'coming off together'. For Lawrence apparently made the risky empirical assumption—but perhaps the general and critical reaction to the work is some confirmation—that most people don't know how good sex can be. Hence there is a certain narrowness in the vision of Connie and Mellors' relationship to give Sagar's objection a footing.

However, there is no excuse for critics using obvious faults in the novel to rationalize their scepticism towards its substance. The problem is whether we are dealing with *faults* of intrusive didacticism or a completely unbalanced treatment of, to take the obvious instance, Clifford; yet the feeling that Clifford has been treated unfairly may derive from suspicion of the sexual material. After all, as Lawrence himself says dryly, sententiously, in the opening paragraph, 'We've got to live, no matter how many skies have fallen', is not Clifford's adaptation to his misfortune (it might be argued) worthy of some sympathetic recognition? But when the hollowness of the opening platitudes begins to resound, when the casual tone is abandoned and Lawrence's prose develops to its bitterest tenacity:

> Tevershall pit-bank was burning, had been burning for years, and it would cost thousands to put it out. So it had to burn. And when the wind was that way, which was often, the house was full of the stench of this sulphurous combustion of the earth's excrement. But even on windless days the air always smelt of something underearth: sulphur, iron, coal, or acid. And even on the Christmas roses the smuts settled persistently, incredible, like black manna from the skies of doom,

we begin to see what Clifford's adaptation means:

> Well, there it was: fated like the rest of things! It was rather awful, but why kick? You couldn't kick it away. It just went on. Life, like all the rest! ...

Connie's fascination, and sense of mystery in the miners, are signs of life; but getting used to it—'Life, like all the rest'—'why kick?'—is an abdication of response, of responsibility, to Clifford's acceptance of a crippled civilization.

> Clifford professed to like Wragby better than London. This country had a grim will of its own, and the people had guts. Connie wondered what else they had ...

But Connie learns to 'harden' herself to the 'strange denial of the common pulse of humanity'. The horror is not so much in the *fact* of the existence of mines and industry as in the attitude that takes them for granted, that is blind to further possibilities of life: Clifford's attitude.

Thus the opening remarks are an extremely pointed warning of the substance of the novel:

> Ours is essentially a tragic age, so we refuse to take it tragically. The cataclysm has happened, we are among the ruins, we start to build up new little habitats, to have new little hopes. It is rather hard work: there is now no smooth road into the future: but we go round, or scramble over the obstacles. We've got to live—

But how? A didactic novelist would hardly present his basic assumptions with such directness, nor allow the emptiness, the pathetic futility of building up 'new little habitats', to seep through the sententiousness.

Lady Chatterley's Lover may not be a great novel, but it has a peculiar strength of desperation—all the apparent variety and complexity of life stripped down to a starkly basic choice—and the poignant beauty of a frail hope that Connie and Mellors might really have found some way of living in a waste land. It should be obvious that it is more about belief—what sort of faith in life, in man, is possible?—than about the phallus or the horrors of industrialism. Clifford is paralysed with fear because of his failure to believe in himself or anything. The essential logic of this and of the whole of the novel is sketched in Chapter I with the same deceptively casual, but ruthless, economy of the opening paragraphs. As one of the 'flannel-trousers Cambridge intransigents' Clifford had ridiculed everything, including the very authority he is landed with on his father's death. It is all a joke turned nasty, like the war; he marries because, as Sagar very aptly says, 'he needed someone to believe in him before he knew he existed'. His adaptation to his lot is a repudiation of individual responsibility and integrity, seeing the individual as insignificant in the society, nation, civilization, 'tradition', 'fate', in which he happens to exist. It is tantamount to saying that life is a meaningless flux, without continuity or purpose. The novel dramatizes with compelling logic the diverging developments of Clifford's and Connie's conditions to their final utter opposition.

Unlike Clifford's acceptance and self-adaptation, the 'hardening' process that Connie undergoes when she comes to Wragby implies a certain strength, a stoicism, which is to be ground for renewal. As she begins, in Chapter 5, to recognize that the 'nothingness' of her life with Clifford derives from his inward emptiness and compensating egoism, the possibilities of new growth are suggested through the imagery associated with the wood and the gamekeeper. But those possibilities are not arbitrarily introduced; they emerge as a different way of seeing things from what Clifford himself values in the wood—the tradition and greatness of the old England that was smashed during the war.

> Clifford loved the wood; he loved the old oak-trees. He felt they were his own through generations. . . .

It is all very beautiful; but there is a clear hint of Clifford's narrowness and possessiveness:

> 'I want this wood perfect . . . untouched. I want nobody to trespass in it,' said Clifford.
> There was a certain pathos. The wood still had some of the mystery of wild, old England; but Sir Geoffrey's cuttings during the war had given it a blow. How still the trees were, with their crinkly, innumerable twigs against the sky, and their grey, obstinate trunks rising from the brown bracken! How safely the birds flitted among them! And once there had been deer, and archers, and monks padding along on asses. The place remembered, still remembered.
> Clifford sat in the pale sun, with the light on his smooth, rather blond hair, his reddish full face inscrutable.
> 'I mind more, not having a son, when I come here, than any other time,' he said.

Nevertheless his desire for a son is there clearly and sympathetically placed. He sees the importance of continuity of the authority he represents:

> 'If some of the old England isn't preserved, there'll be no England at all,' said Clifford. 'And we who have this kind of property, and the feeling for it, *must* preserve it.'
> There was a sad pause.
> 'Yes, for a little while,' said Connie.

Connie's doubt hints at the real threat: she hears the hooters at Stacks

Gate colliery, but 'Clifford was too used to the sound to notice'. He destroys his own position:

'That's why having a son helps; one is only a link in a chain,' he said.
Connie was not keen on chains, but she said nothing. She was think-ing of the curious impersonality of his desire for a son.

Having made his claims for the ruling classes he goes on to say 'I don't believe very intensely in fatherhood' and he proposes a child by another man—who, does not matter. What, then, is the 'tradition' behind his aristocracy? It can only be a matter of 'property', of money and empty social forms.... Clifford's philosophy, like that of his prototype Skrebensky, is a belief in nothing more than self-preservation.

The well-known scene in Chapter 13 in which Connie and Mellors push Clifford and his motor-chair up the hill seems to me less successful than that above—the fine poise is sacrificed to an unneces-sary clarity of statement, and the symbolism becomes a little obtrusive —but it has a strength of certainty (an assurance which makes it only too easy for Lawrence to preach) in taking Clifford's philosophy to its logical conclusion.

'I don't care who his father may be, so long as he is a healthy man not below normal intelligence.... It is not who begets us, that matters, but where fate places us.... Aristocracy is a function, a part of fate. And the masses are a functioning of another part of fate. The individual hardly matters. It is a question of which func-tion you are brought up and adapted to... the function determines the individual.'

Life is reduced to material and mechanical elements, a matter of function to no discernible end, of a veneer of social organization over a random and meaningless 'fate'. At the end, Clifford quite insanely refuses Connie a divorce so that 'the decency and order of life is preserved'. In Chapter 5 he makes apparently more rational claims for 'the steadily-lived life' in two speeches which are masterpieces of Lawrentian satire, and yet which derive from what Clifford sees in the wood, Connie senses something wrong, but failing to put her finger on it, agrees with the reservation that 'life may turn quite a new face on it all'—and Mellors enters right on cue with 'swift menace'.

Clifford does not believe in fatherhood, i.e. in the potency, integrity and authority to back his power, which then is just money-domination and the sheer egoistic will he exhibits in his motor-chair or under the subtle instigation of Mrs Bolton. A society not based on an ethic of the intrinsic significance of individual life is 'mechanical':

This is history. One England blots out another. The mines had made the halls wealthy. Now they were blotting them out, as they had already blotted out the cottages. The industrial England blots out the agricultural England. One meaning blots out another. The new England blots out the old England. And the continuity is not organic but mechanical.

For its 'tradition' is merely a functional repetition of empty forms, *habits*—

'We have the habit of each other. And habit, to my thinking, is more vital than any occasional excitement. The long, slow, enduring thing ... that's what we live by ...'

Clifford's whole philosophy is a rationalization of his sense of his own insignificance as a link in a meaningless chain of time, 'half past eight instead of half past seven'. Hence his persistent egoism and increasing dependence, first on Connie, then on popular fame, and the flattery of his peers, then, childishly, on Mrs Bolton, the mother-figure (nurse) from industrial Teyershall. This is the *reductio ad absurdum*: the rulers, failing to believe in their own potency, become slaves to the masses, needing maternal recognition and reassurance.

And he would gaze on her with wide, childish eyes, in a relaxation of madonna-worship. It was sheer relaxation on his part, letting go all his manhood, and sinking back to a childish position that was really perverse. And then he would put his hand into her bosom and feel her breasts, and kiss them in exultation, the exultation of perversity, of being a child when he was a man.

The vision is so horrifying because the logic of it is so irresistible. The ruler, determined by his function, prostrating himself before society, is not a man but a 'tool'.

The sexual candour of *Lady Chatterley's Lover* is thus brilliantly vindicated as the core of the whole thematic structure of the novel: for a 'tool' is exactly what Connie wants until she learns by bitter frustration with Michaelis that she herself must 'yield'. Again the basic logic is dryly outlined in Chapter I. Disillusioned by their first love-affairs, the sisters decide that what they really want is 'the beautiful pure freedom of a woman'; their motive of being is emancipation—'to shake off the old and sordid connexions and subjections'. But self-realization and egoism are very close; the female ideal of freedom turns into a demand for sexual domination (in its extreme form, the behaviour of Bertha Coutts with Mellors):

... a woman could yield to a man without yielding her inner, free self.... A woman could take a man without really giving herself away. Certainly she could take him without giving herself into his power. Rather she could use this sex thing to have power over him. For she had only to hold herself back in sexual intercourse, and let him finish and expend himself without herself coming to the crisis: and then she could prolong the connexion and achieve her orgasm and her crisis while he was merely her tool.

What is stated so bluntly here is explored with great subtlety and imaginative power in *The Rainbow* and *Women in Love*—such that the failure of even Lawrence's best critics to appreciate the significance of these 'offences against taste' when it *is* stated so bluntly is all the more disturbing. In effect it is the crux of *Lady Chatterley's Lover* and of Lawrence's artistic vision: we see the significance of it when Connie 'comes off together' with Mellors and resolves to relinquish her 'hard bright female power' to which the man would be merely 'phallus bearer' (cf. 'Moony' and Ursula on the beach with Skrebensky).

Connie's affair with Michaelis (a scaled-down Loerke) is a reversal of life. He has a kind of inverted faith, being at such an extreme of disillusionment and cynicism that he is 'pure', with the knowingness of ancient, bitter experience. While he has a thick-skinned toughness far beyond Clifford in honestly accepting cynicism as the measure of things, it follows that his sense of his own insignificance goes much deeper than Clifford's, and in the end he cannot quite sustain it, he has not that kind of stoic strength. He comes to Connie for 'comfort and soothing', for which he is 'poignantly grateful'. In effect then, he arouses Connie's (hitherto unaroused) maternal instincts, or rather, maternal ego, since that is the way he appeals to her and the way she sees him—it is a powerful blend of his erotic invitation and her maternal solicitude ... Michaelis prostitutes himself to Connie just as he prostitutes himself to the 'bitch-goddess, Success'. His total energy is used in 'heroically' keeping himself 'present in her', keeping himself *there*; he is incapable of creative activity. He has insufficient strength to satisfy the mixture of eroticism and 'compassion' he arouses by his prostitution, so she uses him for masturbation.

Despite the temporary thrill and confidence Connie gets from Michaelis (which stimulates Clifford), something of his hopelessness rubs off on her: 'everything in her world and life seemed worn out, and her dissatisfaction was older than the hills.' Michaelis has nothing to offer but the inevitable disillusionment. The 'sad dog' turns savage and destroys her superficial confidence, denigrating the only apparently real thing Connie has had to cling to for her 'freedom', and she accepts the 'great nothingness of life'. Lesson one is finished: 'We've got to live, no matter how many skies have fallen'—'one must live and learn'—it is a grim, bitter lesson:

All that really remained was a stubborn stoicism: and in that there was a certain pleasure. In the very experience of the nothingness of life, phase after phase, *étape* after *étape*, there was a certain grisly satisfaction. So that's *that*! Always this was the last utterance: home, love, marriage, Michaelis: So that's *that*! And when one died, the last words to life would be: So that's *that*!

But the hardening process has been undergone: she has given up all hope of her egoistic 'freedom'. She makes up her mind she wants nothing out of life further except perhaps the experiment of having a baby.

The gradual development of Connie's condition is very moving, the finest part of the novel, accomplishing something that even *The Rainbow* (deeply concerned with continuity as it is) only stabs at in its last chapters: the slow inevitability of a process that is at once decay and growth. The movement is almost imperceptible, but of crucial significance: something like the Ancient Mariner's change of heart between cursing and blessing creation ... Connie ... in resigning herself to the nothingness ... finds a relaxation which is the beginning of new awareness of the life around her—first, of the wood, which is in a similar state of existence, waiting for a spring it does not anticipate:

> In the wood all was utterly inert and motionless, only great drops fell from the bare boughs, with a hollow little crash. For the rest, among the old trees was depth within depth of grey, hopeless inertia, silence, nothingness.
> Connie walked dimly on. From the old wood came an ancient melancholy, somehow soothing to her, better than the harsh insentience of the outer world. She liked the *inwardness* of the remnant of forest, the unspeaking reticence of the old trees. They seemed a very power of silence, and yet a vital presence. They, too, were waiting: obstinately, stoically waiting, and giving off a potency of silence. Perhaps they were only waiting for the end; to be cut down, cleared away, the end of the forest, for them the end of all things. But perhaps their strong and aristocratic silence, the silence of strong trees, meant something else.

Emerging from despair, this beautiful poise or suspension becomes the feature of *Lady Chatterley's Lover* (far transcending any crudity or didacticism): living, despite the 'cataclysm', continuity, is possible but by no means certain.

Connie discovers the virtue of not trying to force things and is rewarded with the visionary shock of seeing the single other life of Mellors—the intrinsic significance of the individual—as Sagar says,

> Here is something which does not throw out the old question—what's the point of it all?—something which ... cannot be mistaken for show, façade, nothingness.

With the timely aid of Mrs Bolton, she disentangles herself from Clifford and comes compulsively to the wood: 'being so still and alone, she seemed to get into the current of her own proper destiny.' She is attracted by Mellors' reserved isolation, his 'stillness' and 'patience'; watching him work, 'she felt almost irresponsible'. She is being relieved of the burden of self-consciousness and self-determination, learning how to 'yield' in the full sense.

To this situation the newly-hatched pheasant chickens are catalysts:

> Life, life! Pure, sparky, fearless new life! New life! So tiny and so utterly without fear! Even when it scampered a little, scrambling into the coop again, and disappeared under the hen's feathers in answer to the mother hen's wild alarm-cries, it was not really frightened, it took it as a game, the game of living. For in a moment a tiny sharp head was poking through the gold-brown feathers of the hen, and eyeing the Cosmos.
>
> Connie was fascinated. And at the same time, never had she felt so acutely the agony of her own female forlornness. It was becoming unbearable.

This is a far cry from the frustrated maternalism we saw in operation with Michaelis. The sense of forces in life beyond and outside man steadily evoked through the timeless strength of the wood is here momentarily crystallized—what life is like for someone who is prepared to trust it:

> She stood the little drab thing between her hands, and there it stood, on its impossible little stalks of legs, its atom of balancing life trembling through its almost weightless feet into Connie's hands. But it lifted its handsome, clean-shaped little head boldly, and looked sharply round, and gave a little 'peep'.

It is itself, and unashamed—just what Connie is not—boldly 'eyeing the Cosmos', absurdly unafraid of life.

Connie cries 'in all the anguish of her generation's forlornness', abandoning her upper-class control in front of her husband's servant, relying on 'the common pulse of humanity', and thus arousing his 'bowels of compassion'. In his desire for her the man assumes responsibility—the power to make life right for Connie is his. Yet Mellors is himself 'helplessly desirous': 'His face was pale and without expression, like that of a man submitting to fate.' Subsequently, while he recognizes the burden of responsibility he has implicitly accepted, he realizes that this is a part of essential life-processes from which he has tried to cut himself off:

> 'There's no keeping clear. And if you do keep clear you might almost as well die. So if I've got to be broken open again, I have.'

And Sagar puts it well:

> When he puts out his hand to a woman in need of love, he is exposing

himself once more to betrayal. But the instinct to give without reservation, to offer one's body with all its emotions and faculties instead of some formula of words, is stronger than the instinct of self-preservation, of distrust.

All he has to offer is a 'blind instinctive caress'—but what else is there? For Connie to regain self-control by any means would be to start all over again. She has perceived finally that life exists and continues quite beyond and outside her *self*, and that she must give herself up to *it*, to the 'unknown' that Tom and Ursula Brangwen distinguish themselves by confronting. She 'yields' not so much to the man as a person as to the forces manifested through him and his desire. She 'could strive for herself no more'—the description is finely balanced between a sense of great peace and the knowledge of how easily it can be broken.

And she knew, if she gave herself to the man, it was real. But if she kept herself for herself, it was nothing. She was old: millions of years old, she felt. And at last, she could bear the burden of herself no more. She was to be had for the taking. To be had for the taking.

The conventional phrase captures the marvellous ironic ambiguity of the scene: her 'modern woman's brain' ('Was it real? Was it real?') reflecting on the depths to which she has socially sunk; and the true significance of the event—in giving herself up to life, she discovers life, and peace.

Much of the subsequent 'persistent indulgence in copulation' is to test Connie's new perception; and there are failures when she is afraid of the man's passion and holds herself back, maintaining self-consciousness, feeling some contempt for him and his 'ridiculous performance'. However, it is now a matter not of discovery but of inward resistance to a force emphatically there, magnificently realized in the prose:

She quivered again at the potent inexorable entry inside her, so strange and terrible. It might come with the thrust of a sword in her softly-opened body, and that would be death. She clung in a sudden anguish of terror. But it came with a strange slow thrust of peace, the dark thrust of peace and a ponderous, primordial tenderness, such as made the world in the beginning. And her terror subsided in her breast, her breast dared to be gone in peace, she held nothing. She dared to let go everything, all herself, and be gone in the flood.

And it seemed she was like the sea, nothing but dark waves rising and heaving, heaving with a great swell, so that slowly her whole darkness was in motion, and she was ocean rolling its dark, dumb mass . . .

In giving way to it she achieves her 'consummation'. The description is so fine because it does not work in terms of the consciously observed sensation (which would tend to be obscenity) but of the whole psychic and physical experience. But it should be clear now how suspicion of Lawrence's 'doctrine' of 'salvation by sex'—or suspicion of the sex itself—can thwart response to the art. For his point is simple enough: it is through sexual relationships that man is most directly confronted with the universe, Nature, the whole unknown other life beyond his egoistic consciousness—but only if he is prepared to trust himself and those forces, to give himself up to them. The fear of sex (Clifford) and the selfish use of it (Connie and Michaelis) amount to a distrust of life.

It is at this point that the novel might be seen to break down into an idyllic celebration of sexual fulfilment or an 'insistent, obsessive sexuality'. Any further development rests squarely on Mellors. For the great reserves of potency suggested in the wood, the strength of which Mellors shares while he maintains his enigmatic isolation, have to be translated into human terms if 'continuity' is to mean anything: Mellors must be more than gamekeeper, preserver of life 'to be shot ultimately by fat men after breakfast'. The faults of the later part of the novel—again they are *faults* of insistence and self-justification, implying doubt, not (with one possible exception) ruinously narrow didacticism—reflect Lawrence's uncertainty as to what Mellors has to offer Connie beyond being a 'phallus-bearer', a gigolo, Lady Chatterley's lover. They reflect, that is, the central preoccupation of the novel as the title implies. The slight unreality about Mellors' dual personality is compensated for by an occasional emphasis on the symbollic phallus, and self-conscious sign-posting of the natural innocence and freedom of the love, by making Mellors' approval of Connie's 'tail' into a symbol, by increasing the virulence of the attacks on industrialism and the 'mental life' of Clifford, and so on. Ironically, the insistence on Connie's achievement of unashamed nakedness (on the night before she leaves for Venice) hits a note of exultance reminiscent of her 'hard bright female power'. But when the problem of the future is faced and dramatized openly, the novel maintains its fine poise between faith and despair.

Mellors admits that 'he was temporizing with life . . . for he did not know what to do with himself'. While he rationalizes slightly—the fault, we find, is not in his despair, purposelessness and misanthropy, but out there in the world where all anybody cares about is money —the situation, the crucial test of Mellors' life, is unhesitatingly contemplated. For Mellors, as for most of Lawrence's major male characters, sexual fulfilment is not complete fulfilment; indeed it seems to give him only a kind of weariness that he has to bother at all about the future. The world being what it is, his only hope is the same

negative compromise Lawrence himself made, as do Birkin, Lilly and
Somers: to become a wanderer on the face of the earth.

> It was insoluble. He could only think of going to America, to try
> a new air. He disbelieved in the dollar utterly. But perhaps, perhaps
> there was something else.

A barren hope, reflected in the pathos of the end of the novel. In
fact it is a barren world, a barren life: love is not so much an answer
to it as a refuge from it like the wood:

> It was a world of iron and coal, the cruelty of iron and the smoke
> of coal, and the endless, endless greed that drove it all. Only greed,
> greed stirring in its sleep.
> It was cold, and he was coughing. A fine cold draught blew over
> the knoll. He thought of the woman. Now he would have
> given all he had or ever might have to hold her warm in his arms,
> both of them wrapped in one blanket, and sleep. All hopes of etern-
> ity and all gain from the past he would have given to have her there,
> to be wrapped warm with him in one blanket, and sleep, only
> sleep. It seemed the sleep with the woman in his arms was the only
> necessity.

That sadness and weariness is very close to the feeling of the whole
novel, if one can talk of such things, very close to Lawrence himself:
and the phallus has been forgotten.

The scene in the hut in the rain (Chapter 15—not the laugh-
able failure it is often made out to be) is something of a crisis, for Connie
announces her probable pregnancy. Mellors admits that he has no hope
for the future:

> 'Why,' he said at last, 'It seems to me a wrong and bitter thing to do,
> to bring a child into this world.'
> 'No! Don't say it! Don't say it!' she pleaded. 'I think I'm going to
> have one. Say you'll be pleased.' She laid her hand on his.
> 'I'm pleased for you to be pleased,' he said. 'But for me it seems a
> ghastly treachery to the unborn creature.'
> 'Ah no!' she said, shocked. 'Then you *can't* ever really want me!
> You *can't* want me, if you feel that!'
> Again he was silent, his face sullen. Outside there was only the
> threshing of the rain.

His silence is almost tacit agreement; but the rain makes the general
point anyway—what future is there? Perhaps a good Old Testament
flood in the style of *The Rainbow* or *The Virgin and the Gypsy* to
clean things up. If there is a future it is utterly inscrutable; any
faith must come from within, and Mellors here cannot muster it.
Connie tries to blackmail him with love, finding an excuse for his

bitterness; he plaintively, idly dreams of men in red trousers, significantly lapsing into the brogue:

> 'It's not quite true!' she whispered. 'It's not quite true! There's another truth!' She felt he was bitter now partly because she was leaving him, deliberately going away to Venice. And this half pleased her.
>
> She pulled open his clothing and uncovered his belly, and kissed his navel. Then she laid her cheek on his belly and pressed her arm down his warm, silent loins. They were alone in the flood.
>
> 'Tell me you want a child, in hope!' she murmured, pressing her face against his belly. 'Tell me you do!'
>
> 'Why!' he said at last: and she felt the curious quiver of changing consciousness and relaxation going through his body. 'Why I've thought sometimes if one but tried, here among th' colliers even! They're workin' bad now, an' not earnin' much. If a man could say to em: Dunna think o' nowt but th' money. When it comes ter *wants*, we want but little. Let's not live for money—'
>
> She softly rubbed her cheek on his belly, and gathered his balls in her hand. The penis stirred softly, with strange life, but did not rise up. The rain beat bruisingly outside.

The rain is unanswerable. There is little phallic strength to support Mellors' sermon—Lawrence is not deceiving himself even if Mellors is. It is not surprising that the little ceremony with the flowers—clearly intended to stand for some sort of mutual commitment or marriage before Connie goes to Venice—seems pathetically, if innocently, inadequate. Mellors believes in fatherhood no more than Clifford does, if for a different reason; and he is only less cynical and disillusioned than Michaelis in refusing to prostitute himself. What price 'organic continuity'?

In the last love scene the question is tackled quite explicitly and things begin to go seriously wrong. The challenge is again Connie's pregnancy. 'Living is moving and moving on' says Mellors, but he can see nowhere to move to ... Mellors becomes evasive. The question shifts to a consideration of what Mellors has 'that other men don't have, and that will make a future.' Connie supplies the predictable answer: 'the courage of your own tenderness ... Like when you put your hand on my tail and say I've got a pretty tail', and Lawrence takes over:

> 'Ay!' he said. 'You're right. It's that really ... It's a question of awareness, as Buddha said. But even he fought shy of the bodily awareness, and that natural physical tenderness, which is the best even between men; in a proper manly way. ... Sex is really only touch, the closest of all touch. And it's touch we're afraid of. ... We've got to come alive and aware. Especially the English have

got to get in touch with one another, a bit delicate and a bit tender.
It's our crying need.'

Having got that in, Lawrence shifts away to the thing he has done
so well in the novel, the tenderness itself: but it looks very like a
subtle form of sentimental escapism.

The description of the love-making that follows is the only one
where something goes quite wrong. Connie dictates, Mellors is
plaintively hesitant, the phrase 'bowels of compassion' is thrown in
for good measure, but tenderness is abandoned for near-hysterical
moralizing:

> . . . 'I stand for the touch of bodily awareness between human
> beings,' he said to himself, 'and the touch of tenderness. And she
> is my mate. And it is a battle against the money, and the machine,
> and the insentient ideal monkeyishness of the world. And she
> will stand behind me there. Thank God I've got a woman! Thank
> God I've got a woman who is with me, and tender and aware of me.
> Thank God she's not a bully, nor a fool. Thank God she's a tender,
> aware woman.' And as his seed sprang in her, his soul sprang to-
> wards her too, in the creative act that is far more than procreative.

The insistently rhythmical 'Thank God . . .' is almost obscene, and
this kind of consciousness is clearly *not* the way 'to come into tender
touch' meaningfully. Mellors' pride, dignity and integrity as a man
remain fragile and questionable to the end of the novel.

In the end, then, Lawrence offers 'tenderness' almost as a panacea
and moralizes his way out of the sharpest challenges to it. All evil is
rationalized into the outside world of industrialism and 'the mental
life'; it is a Garden of Eden story in which no guilt devolves upon the
lovers—they are too innocent to be true. People like Tom Brangwen,
Ursula, Birkin, even Lilly and Somers find they *are* implicated—
they are a part of humanity as much as they try to detach themselves.
Similarly in the great novels Nature is not seen as unambiguously
beneficent; the possibilities of evil and destruction in Nature as in
sex and sensuality, of 'organic continuity' being meaningless, no
continuity at all or aimed at a universal cataclysm, are held firmly in
view.

This is not to say that Lawrence fails to make the tenderness viable;
on the contrary, as we have seen, it is brilliantly and poignantly done.
Poignantly—that is the point: the tenderness itself implies its own
frailty, that it is a substitute for something stronger which is missing.
As realized in *Lady Chatterley's Lover* tenderness is very close to
despairing resignation; and one may feel that Mellors' 'bowels of
compassion' is a little apologetic, confirming the hopelessness it tries
to redeem. And this is far from asserting that the novel is a failure,
being no triumphant affirmation of life; again on the contrary, from

this point of view it is a powerful if saddening work. What failure
there is, is in the phallus: it simply does not do the job expected of
it, it is not a bridge into the future as Tommy Dukes says:

> 'Our old show will come flop; our civilization is going to fall. It's
> going down the bottomless pit, down the chasm. And believe me,
> the only bridge across the chasm will be the phallus!'

However, it is a straw to cling to.

Hence the ending of *Lady Chatterley's Lover* is all pathos. We have
a very narrow and limited faith, and a very tentative hope that it might
survive for a little while, despite Mellors' insistence that 'all the bad
times that have ever been, haven't been able to blow the crocus out;
not even the love of women'. But Mellors cannot quite believe in
himself fully; neither, it seems, can Lawrence. Unable to believe in
himself he cannot believe in man. The faith is in sex-as-nature rather
than sex-as-human, which implies a certain failure of human concern,
'bowels of compassion' notwithstanding. Here, then, Lawrence's
misanthropy does get the better of him; and here, as a result, the novel
is less about people than it is about sex. . . .

Yet the years he spent wandering the earth, trying a 'new air', and
experimenting in philosophy and fiction have by no means gone for
nothing—we have the assurance and compelling logic with which
'authority' and 'yielding' are handled to show that. If *Lady Chatterley's Lover* seems a considerable comedown from *The Rainbow* and
Women in Love (which it is, they being very great novels indeed)
if Lawrence seems to have ended up more or less in the position of
Birkin after being biffed on the head by Hermione, preferring the
world of nature to the world of man—nevertheless he has remained
true to the vision of his great novels:

> The same with man. He has to build his own tissue and form,
> serving the community for the means wherewithal, and then he
> comes to the climax. And at the climax, simultaneously, he begins
> to roll to the edge of the unknown, and, in the same moment, lays
> down his seed for security's sake. That is the secret of life: it
> contains the lesser motions in the greater. In love, a man, a woman,
> flows on to the very furthest edge of known feeling, being, and out
> beyond the furthest edge: and taking the superb and supreme
> risk, deposits a security of life in the womb.
> Am I here to deposit security, continuance of life in the flesh? Or is
> that only a minor function in me? Is it not merely a preservative
> measure, procreation? . . .
> It is so arranged that the very act which carried us out into the
> unknown shall probably deposit seed for security to be left behind.
> But the act, called the sexual act, is not for the depositing of the

seed. It is for leaping off into the unknown, as from a cliff's edge, like Sappho into the sea. ('Study of Thomas Hardy', 1914.)

Even if Connie's pregnancy is an unconvincing guarantee of security, she and Mellors do make their little leap. The emphasis should not be left on how narrow and frail a work it is; that the faith, the vision of life, survives despite its frailty and thus proves its viability is the achievement and beauty of the novel.

The Critical Review, University of Melbourne, No. 10, 1967.

H. M. DALESKI

The Tiger and the Lamb:
The Duality of Lawrence

A central feature of Lawrence's thought is its dualism. Lawrence both proclaimed his own duality—'I know I am compound of two waves ... I am framed in the struggle and embrace of the two opposite waves of darkness and of light'[1]—and asserted that 'everything that exists, even a stone, has two sides to its nature'.[2] We are not surprised, therefore, to find that his interpretation of the large movement of history should be expressed in these terms:

'We must never forget that mankind lives by a twofold motive: the motive of peace and increase, and the motive of contest and martial triumph. As soon as the appetite for martial adventure and triumph in conflict is satisfied, the appetite for peace and increase manifests itself, and vice versa. It seems a law of life.'[3]

Similarly, Lawrence detects in 'nearly all great novelists' a dichotomy of a 'didactic purpose ... directly opposite to their passional inspiration'.[4] He also distinguishes between the Old and New Testaments in terms of the Holy Spirit which manifests itself both as a Dove (the New Testament) and as an Eagle,[5] and maintains that Christianity itself is dual, being both a 'religion of the strong, [that teaches] renunciation and love', and a 'religion of the weak, [that teaches] down with the strong and the powerful, and let the poor be glorified'.[6]

I do not wish to suggest that Lawrence invariably clamped diverse generalizations into the vice of a dualistic thesis. Statements such as those I have just quoted were rather the natural ambience of a constant position, and in the expository writings which deal specifically with his theory of duality he is for the best part content to make his point metaphorically or symbolically. That is to say, duality is viewed as an all-pervading principle, but no attempt is made to demonstrate or

[1] 'The Crown', *Reflections on the Death of a Porcupine* (Philadelphia, 1925), p. 24.
[2] '... Love Was Once a Little Boy', *Reflections*, p. 183.
[3] *Movements in European History*, pseud. Lawrence H. Davison (London, 1921), p. 306.
[4] 'The Novel', *Reflections*, p. 105. See too *Studies in Classic American Literature* (New York, 1923), *passim*.
[5] *Twilight in Italy* (London, 1916), p. 29.
[6] *Apocalypse* (London, 1932), p. 18.

argue the intuition systematically. Instead, the opposed forces are seen symbolically, in terms of the dark and the light, the eagle and the dove, the tiger and the lamb, or the lion and the unicorn. What is insisted on, however, time and again, is both the fact of opposition and the necessity for its existence, to the point indeed of turning the conflict into a *raison d'être*: [The lion and the unicorn] would both cease to be, if either of them really won in the fight [for the crown] which is their sole reason for existing',[7] and 'Homer was wrong in saying, "Would that strife might pass away from among gods and men!" He did not see that he was praying for the destruction of the universe; for in the tension of opposites all things have their being.'[8] It is this concept of the tension of opposites and the relation which Lawrence wishes to see established between the contending forces that have a direct bearing on his art.

It is not easy to describe the nature of the relation precisely since Lawrence expresses his intuitions symbolically. 'Phoenix, Crown, Rainbow, Plumed Serpent', writes Henry Miller, 'all ... centre about the same obsessive idea: the resolution of two opposites in the form of a mystery.'[9] The selection of symbols is illuminating, but the word 'resolution', in so far as it implies a dissolution of the opposites, is misleading. The end product is a mystery—it is a unified whole created out of discordant elements—but what distinguishes Lawrence's position from most dualist philosophies in his insistence that the contending forces must retain their separate identities. The new whole which is created by establishing a relation between the opposites is not a fusing of the two into one but a complementing of the one by the other; and the relation itself is the only absolute Lawrence is prepared to acknowledge ...

Lawrence views relationship between individuals in much the same way. I have avoided using the word 'balance' to describe what is really a recurring movement from one extreme to the other of forces within

---

[7] 'The Crown', *Reflections*, p. 3. Cf. Blake in 'The Marriage of Heaven and Hell': 'Without contraries is no progression. Attraction and Repulsion, Reason and Energy, Love and Hate, are necessary to Human existence.' F. R. Leavis was the first, in this respect, to point out the 'significant parallel' between Lawrence's thought and that of Blake; see 'D. H. Lawrence', *For Continuity* (Cambridge, 1933), pp. 111–13.

[8] 'Notes for *Birds, Beasts and Flowers*', *Phoenix*, p. 67. Cf. 'War, then, is the father and king of all things, in the world as in human society; and Homer's wish that strife might cease was really a prayer for the destruction of the world.' John Burnet, *Early Greek Philosophy* (London, 1920), p. 164. Though Lawrence was interested in Burnet as early as 1916—see Edward Nehls, *D. H. Lawrence: A Composite Biography*, Vol. I (Madison, 1957), p. 402—there is no evidence that he had read Early Greek Philosophy when he first formulated his theory of duality in works such as *Twilight in Italy* and the 'Study of Thomas Hardy'. I am inclined to believe that Lawrence's dualistic outlook was primarily the result of his own early experience—see p. 73 below—and that he turned later to the Greek philosophers for confirmation of his ideas.

[9] 'Creative Death', *The Wisdom of the Heart* (London 1947), p. 10.

the individual, but it aptly suggests the counterpoise which Lawrence believes to be necessary in personal relations. Where the relationship is that between a man and a woman, there is a double reconciliation of opposites, for the man and the woman are required not only to meet as opposites but, as we have seen, to reconcile the opposing qualities within themselves. The relationship is envisaged as a meeting on equal terms of two people who have themselves achieved full individuality and transcend their duality in the balance that is attained between them:

'If it is to be life then it is fifty per cent me, fifty per cent thee: and the third thing, the spark, which springs from out of the balance, is timeless. Jesus, who saw it a bit vaguely, called it the Holy Ghost. 'Between man and woman, fifty per cent man and fifty per cent woman: then the pure spark. Either this, or less than nothing.'[10]

The duality of male and female is central to Lawrence's dualism and requires separate consideration. Lawrence's major pronouncement on this subject is to be found in the 'Study of Thomas Hardy' (1914).[11]

In the Hardy essay Lawrence is not otherwise inconsistent in his discussion of the attributes of male and female, but the scattered multiplication of instances tends to be confusing. I have therefore abstracted the qualities which are enumerated and present them in the following table:

Male	Female
Movement	Stability
Change	Immutability
Activity	Permanence
Time	Eternality
Will-to-Motion	Will-to-Inertia
Registers Relationships	Occupied in Self-Feeling
Refusal of Sensation	Submission to Sensation
Multiplicity and Diversity	Oneness
Knowledge	Feeling
Love	Law
Spirit	Flesh
God the Son	God the Father
Service of Some Idea	Full Life in the Body
Doing	Being
Self-Subordination	Self-Establishment
Utterance	Gratification in the Senses
Abstraction	
Public Good	Enjoyment through the Senses

[10] 'Him with His Tail in His Mouth', *Reflections*, p. 141.

[11] Cf. 'I am just finishing a book, supposed to be on Thomas Hardy, but in reality a sort of Confessions of my Heart. I wonder if ever it will come out. . . .' Letter to Amy Lowell (November 1914), S. Foster Damon, *Amy Lowell: A Chronicle* (New York, 1935), p. 279.

Male	Female
Community	
Mental Clarity	Sensation
Consciousness	Instinct
Spirit	Soul
Mind	Senses
Consciousness	Feelings
Knowledge	Nature
Condition of Knowledge	Condition of Being
Brain	Body
Stalk	Root
Light	Darkness
Movement towards Discovery	Movement towards the Origin

It is unlikely that psychologists would find these distinctions acceptable; but this is not the point at issue. The classification serves as a useful index to Lawrence's thought, and there are several inferences which can be drawn from it. In the first place, it seems clear that the male-female duality is at the heart of his dualistic beliefs. Graham Hough firmly denies this: 'The Male-Female opposition is an instance of this duality [i.e., 'dual reality'] but only an instance; and Lawrence is not constructing the world on the model of sexual duality. The Father, for example, is on the same side as the female.' [*The Dark Sun*, p. 225.] That the Father is an instance of the female principle is admittedly paradoxical but not by itself inconsistent; indeed, it may be argued that this is an indication of the extent to which Lawrence does construct the world on the model of male-female duality. The male-female opposition is not merely an instance of a dual reality but its underlying principle . . .

The Forked Flame, London, 1965, pp. 20–31.

EUGENE GOODHEART

The Man Who Died

The Man Who Died[1] is the masterpiece of Lawrence's 'final period', the period in which Lawrence conceived the new 'reciprocity of tenderness'. It is a kind of grand summation of Lawrence's principal themes, a revelation of the strengths and weaknesses of his utopian ambitions.

The Man Who Died begins on an ironic note. Lawrence's Christ is miraculously recalled to life by a 'loud and splitting' cock crow. Pained and disillusioned, the man discovers that the world that he had denied for the illusory glory of eternal life has its own undying glory. 'The world, the same as ever, the natural world, thronging with greenness, a nightingale singing winsomely, wistfully, coaxingly calling from the bushes beside a runnel of water, in the world, the natural world of morning and evening, forever undying, from which he had died.'

With his keen religious intuition, Lawrence has subtly perceived the religious heresy of the Christian impulse toward self-transcendence. By trying to exceed the reach of his hands and feet in order to achieve communion with God—in order perhaps to become God—man is separated from God and diminished in the separation. The nausea, the emptiness and disillusion that the man who died suffers are the 'rewards' Lawrence imagines for the sacrilege. Lawrence is presenting in a new way the old paradox of the Christian critique of the Renaissance conception of man—namely, that the centring of the universe around man makes for a diminution of his stature. As Lawrence exploits the paradox, however, man in his full splendour and potency is conceived by Lawrence according to the Renaissance model. For Lawrence, as for every true religious writer, the imagination of divinity and the imagination of the self are inextricably bound together. As the imagination of divinity fails, so does the imagination of the self. Lawrence's loathing of modern literature derives from a feeling that it offers us the spectacle of small selves in a godless universe, attempting to achieve significance through the magnification of their most trivial feelings. ('... it is self-consciousness, picked into such fine bits that the bits are most of them invisible, and you have to go by the smell. Through thousands and thousands of pages Mr Joyce and Mrs Richardson tear themselves to pieces, strip their emotions to the finest threads.'[2])

[1] *The Man Who Died* was not Lawrence's title; in editions published during his lifetime the book had its true title *The Escaped Cock*.

[2] *Phoenix*, p. 518.

The effect of Lawrence's contempt for 'the idiotic foot-rule' that 'man is the measure of the universe'[3] is a kind of misanthropy. In *The Man Who Died*, for instance, the repudiation of Christ's mission to convert men to the God of Love ('to lay the compulsion of love on all men') is accompanied by an intense hatred of the City of Man.

> So he went on his way, and was alone. But the way of the world was past belief, as he saw the strange entanglement of passions and circumstance and compulsion everywhere, but always the dread insomnia compulsion. It was fear, the ultimate fear of death, that made men mad. So always he must move on, for if he stayed, his neighbours wound the strangling of their fear and bullying around him. There was nothing he could touch, for all, in a mad assertion of ego, wanted to put a compulsion on him, and violate his intrinsic solitude. It was the mania of cities and societies and hosts, to lay a compulsion upon a man, upon all men. For men and women alike are mad with the egoistic fear of their own nothingness.[4]

We are reminded in the above passage of Lawrence's kinship with other misanthropes: Swift and Nietzsche, for example. The misanthropy is obviously connected with Lawrence's attraction to the 'inhuman' and the 'impersonal': the cosmic energy before individuation in its condition of mystery. Throughout his work there is a fascination with the undomesticated 'inhuman' quality of his characters.

The action of *The Man Who Died* is the painful recovery of the God in the body, which culminates in the man's passionate embrace of the priestess of Isis. The fierce and raging physical life that had earlier seemed resistant now responds to their passion.

> All changed, the blossom of the universe changed its petals and swung round to look another way. The spring was fulfilled, a contact was established, the man and the woman were fulfilled of one another.[5]

Significantly, the priestess of Isis is abandoned at the end of *The Man Who Died*, having fulfilled her role as the conduit to the mysteries of 'the greater life of the body'.

If Lawrence is averse to Christianity, there remains nonetheless his

---

[3] In a letter to Trigant Burrow, Lawrence writes the following: 'People are too dead and too conceited. Man is the measure of the universe. Let him be it: idiotic foot-rule which even then is nothing. In my opinion, one can never know: and never-never understand. One can but swim like a trout in a quick stream . . .' (*The Letters of D. H. Lawrence*, p. 635). This is a very compressed statement of Lawrence's view of the humanist presumption. The fatality of consciousness is that it separates man from the world, compels him to regard himself, and makes the moment of self-regard, as it were, the meaning of the world.

[4] *The Man Who Died*, in *The Short Novels*, II, 22.   [5] *Ibid.*, p. 44.

deep attraction to the figure of Christ. Lawrence's Christ retains the chastity, the purity of soul that marks the Christ of the gospels. Before his embrace of the priestess of Isis there had been a long and difficult 'rebirth', in which the man had learned 'the irrevocable noli me tangere which separates the reborn from the vulgar'. Christ's misguided chastity is turned into a strength. Like the other Laurentian heroes, Aaron and Somers, the man who died must resist the lure of false, self-diminishing connections. Before his meeting with the priestess of Isis, he undergoes a kind of purification in which he relives his old experiences—with humanity . . . with Madeleine, with Judas. (The purification recalls Blake's aphorism in 'The Marriage of Heaven and Hell': 'If the doors of perception were cleansed everything would appear to man as it is, infinite.'[6])

The tenderness between the man and the priestess is not the sentimentalism of a new love code. The touch of the priestess heals the man's wounds, but more than that it connects the man with the living universe and restores to him a sense of power. Indeed, the fulfilment between the man and the priestess is short-lived, for 'departure was in the air'. And the man's departing words to the priestess recall the insistence in *Fantasia of the Unconscious* on the necessity of the daylight world, where a man can be with other men or alone on the frontier of the unknown.

'I must go now soon. Trouble is coming to me from the slaves. But I am a man, and the world is open. But what is between us is good, and is established. Be at peace. And when the nightingale calls again from your valley-bed, I shall come again, sure as spring.'[7]

Though the man 'would go alone, with his destiny', the priestess' touch will be upon him and will be, as it were, the bond that guarantees his return to her in the spring.

The aloneness theme persists even at the moment of Lawrence's new imagination of 'the reciprocity of tenderness', and it is the mark of the importance of the preceding phase of Lawrence's career when his people were in sharp recoil from connections with others. The inhuman and nihilistic tendency in Lawrence's work required the check that came from his sensuousness. But the tendency is present in *The Man Who Died*, though in a more humanized form, and the essential egocentricism of Lawrence's imagination is as strong as ever.

'I have sowed the seed of my life and my resurrection, and put my touch forever upon the choice woman of this day, and I carry her perfume in my flesh like essence of roses. She is dear to me in the

[6] William Blake, 'The Marriage of Heaven and Hell', in *The Portable Blake* (New York: Viking Press, 1953), p. 264.

[7] *The Man Who Died*, in *The Short Novels*, II, pp. 45–46.

middle of my being. But the gold and flowing serpent is coiling up again, to sleep at the root of my tree.'[8]

The egocentricism is humanized not only by the sensuousness, but also by a new note of humility. The humility is evident only if one reads *The Man Who Died* as a double allegory on Lawrence himself as well as on Christ. The man's speech to Madeleine, for instance, unmistakably registers a personal note.

'But my mission is over, and my teaching is finished and death has saved me from my own salvation. Oh Madeleine, I want to take my single way in life, which is my portion. My public life is over, the life of my self-importance.'[9]

One cannot avoid having in mind the frail, red-bearded writer with the messianic sense. Lawrence is here rejecting not only Christ's particular mission, but also the self-created legend that had its absurd apotheosis in the notorious 'last supper' at the Café Royale. But if Lawrence assumed the messianic role, he soon learned its bitter fruits. There were plenty of Judases within his own circle, and like the man of the Christ story, Lawrence learned how much he himself was responsible for the betrayals he experienced. There are anticipations of Lawrence's abdication of the messianic role in his letters, admissions that his doctrine of spontaneity and individual being was compromised by the categorical imperatives that he was constantly issuing. In a letter to Lady Cynthia Asquith, Lawrence recognizes his own impulse to lay compulsions upon other people—to dictate his spontaneous feelings to others.

And never again will I say, generally, 'the war'; only 'the war to me'. For to every man the war is himself, and I cannot dictate what the war is or should be to any other being than myself. Therefore I am sorry for all my generalities, which must be falsities to another man, almost insults. Even Rupert Brooke's sonnets which I repudiate for myself, I know how true it is for him, for them.[10]

No art, especially one with a strong prophetic intention, can avoid the 'generalities' which Lawrence vows to eschew. In *Lady Chatterley's Lover*, for instance, though he has presumably given up trying to change the world, the simple presentation of a relationship between lovers reflects Lawrence's urging of a change of consciousness that he would want to become universal. Indeed, art—even when it is most private or when its subject is the most intimate relationships between people—is, because of its public character, an action in the world. An art, however, that springs from acute mistrust of the public world, that has learned the lesson of how the self is compromised in its

[8] *Ibid.*, p. 47.   [9] *Ibid.*, p. 13.
[10] *The Letters of D. H. Lawrence*, p. 379.

action in the world and that chooses in its alienation to cultivate an understanding of the intimate and personal lives of men, is caught on the horns of a dilemma. How is it to protect itself from the consequences of its publicity? Lawrence's savage portrait of Hermione, a 'Laurentian personality', comes out of just such an awareness. And so do the countless letters written during Lawrence's dark period in which he counselled hiding and retreating.

> Shelter yourself above all from the world, save yourself, screen and hide yourself, go subtly in retreat, where no one knows you ... hiding like a bird, and living busily the other creative life, like a bird building a nest....[11]

And yet if the dilemma can never really be resolved, it is nevertheless true that the human activity that suffers least from the dilemma is art, because it is the only human activity that can preserve the 'illusion' of privacy even in its public aspect. 'The single way of life' that the man who died chooses is a choice that we are all urged to make, and as such 'the Mission' has simply taken another form, but 'the compulsion' to choose the single way depends upon the individual reader, who will be moved only if he feels that the man has made the choice out of his own experience and suffering and not as part of the writer's design to persuade him. In other words, the degree to which a work is the incarnation of one's creative life, which for Lawrence takes place in 'hiding', the more powerful will be its effect on the lives of the people it touches.

The ambiguous relationship between Christ and the law gave Lawrence, as it gave Blake and Dostoevsky, a unique opportunity to present his claims for 'the single way of life'. If Christ comes to fulfil the law, he comes also to destroy the version of the law—whatever it may be—that prevails in the world. Blake's Christ assimilates to himself the energies of Hell in order to destroy the life-killing 'rules' that govern the human spirit: 'I tell you, no virtue can exist without breaking these ten commandments. Jesus was all virtue, and acted from impulse, not from rules.'[12] And Dostoevsky's Christ brings the gift of complete spiritual freedom, because the Church which bears His name has taken it away from mankind in exchange for mystery, miracle, and authority. The opposition between Christ and the law in its worldly embodiment is the opposition between vital spirit and dead matter, between freedom and coercion, spontaneity and compulsion. If it is the nature of the world to turn energy into matter, power into weakness, the spirit into the word, then Christ exists as the permanent possibility of the renewal of energy, power, and spirit. Though he has no permanent abode in the world, there is always the possibility of his return.

[11] *Ibid.*, p. 375.
[12] Blake, 'The Marriage of Heaven and Hell', in *The Portable Blake*, p. 258.

H

Indeed, from this point of view even Nietzsche, the great 'antichrist' of modern culture, is, as G. Wilson Knight has pointed out, 'analogous to Christ himself in [Christ's] challenge against the rigidity of Judaic Law'.[13] Knight has very brilliantly argued for the Dionysian, or power, content of Christ's doctrine as opposed to the Christian doctrine. Thus he distinguishes between the inclusive 'super-sexuality' of Christ and 'the ghostly, bloodless, nasalized and utterly unsexual ... tone of our Church tradition'.[14] Jesus' dread of the crowd, his impulse to solitude, and the pain and joy of the crucifixion and resurrection are regarded by Knight as the Dionysian involvement with the cosmos that carries the self beyond the 'normal' sexual and sensual experience of the world into a hermaphroditic oneness of the self with the universe, of the self with the self. Thus Christ's love is not altruism but self-renewal. Viewed from this 'higher critical' position, Lawrence's *The Man Who Died* is a great retelling of the story within the tradition.

But Lawrence's version, in which the man separates himself from the vulgar after he descends from the cross, is a repudiation of something central in the Christian ethos. Lawrence has seen through the willed democratic character of Christianity and rejected it for a fierce aristocratic aloneness. Whatever ultimate significance the life of Jesus had—and it is reasonable to regard Jesus himself as in a sense anti-Christian—Christianity for writers like Blake, Nietzsche, and Lawrence had come to be an enemy of life, and the attempts of commentators and critics to reconcile them to Christianity on some higher ground have the effect of depriving them of the weapon that Jesus himself was permitted: the sword. Like Christ, Lawrence came with the sword. His message was not peace and reconciliation, but destruction and re-creation. The gentle Jesus who embodied the hopes and aspirations of the meek and the poor (the Jesus of Christianity) is an alien spirit to Lawrence.

In an introduction that Lawrence wrote to Dostoevsky's version of the Christ story, the un-Christian and aristocratic power bias of Lawrence's imagination is confirmed in an extraordinary way. In summarizing the argument of the Grand Inquisitor, Lawrence makes his characteristic effort to rescue the tale from the artist. According to Lawrence, Christ's kiss, which is paralleled in the Karamazov story by the kiss Ivan receives from Alyosha, is a kiss of acquiescence in the rightness of the Grand Inquisitor's argument. 'Ivan had made a rediscovery of a truth that had been lost since the eighteenth century.'[15] The truth, which puts the lie to the rationalist belief in the perfectibility of all men, is that the burden of freedom can be

[13] Knight, *Christ and Nietzsche*, p. 119.
[14] *Ibid.*, p. 210.
[15] Introduction to 'The Grand Inquisitor', *Phoenix*, p. 290.

endured by the gifted, unhappy few who must assume the burden
for the rest of mankind. Lawrence very shrewdly observes that the
Grand Inquisitor's argument is close to the Christian idea of a single
man supremely endowed, assuming the burden for all mankind. But
we are kept from seeing the resemblance by the dramatic situation,
the 'cynical Satanical' pose that the Grand Inquisitor is made to affect.
He is presumably in league with the Devil, and the fact that 'the wise
[humane] old man' has been made to put on the garb of the terrible
Inquisitor of the auto-da-fé distracts us from the wisdom and the
humanity of his argument.

Lawrence turns the Grand Inquisitor's argument into a justification
of his mistrust of what Nietzsche calls 'the herd' and of the necessity of protecting the freedom and power of the few from the presumption that all men are capable of perfection.

So let the specially gifted few make the decision between good and
evil and establish the life values against the money values. And let
the many accept the decision, with gratitude, and bow down to the
few, in the hierarchy.[16]

Lawrence wrote the article when the political possibility was still
open to him. In *The Man Who Died* the public life is renounced, but
the aristocratic and Nietzschean bias remains.

It is, of course, a curious fact that Lawrence sides with the Grand
Inquisitor against Christ, though for reasons different from those
that explain Lawrence's affinity with Christ elsewhere. There is
throughout Lawrence a fear that the doctrine of spontaneity and freedom will be perverted by those for whom freedom is an excuse for
self-indulgence and coercion. Lawrence's willingness to send
Dostoevsky's Christ away is a salutary warning to his readers of the
danger that his own work embodies. His misanthropy, paradoxically,
keeps him from wanting his doctrine to become the property of all
men. Lawrence's 'political period' immediately preceding *The Man
Who Died* was very instructive in this respect. The hero of
Kangaroo, for instance, learns that he must repudiate political connections that will violate his singleness. There is a qualifying humility in
Lawrence (a consequence of his religious character perhaps) which
keeps him from sharing Blake's and Nietzsche's belief in the power
of men (even the best of them) to transcend themselves infinitely.
Lawrence mistrusted what Mark Schorer has called (writing of Blake)
the politics of vision. His respect for human limitations counteracted
the anarchic Dionysian tendency of his imagination. His work at
moments seems a balance of opposing tendencies, and this balance
gives the impression of health and normality, which critics like F. R.
Leavis make so much of. Even in Lawrence's fierce repudiations and

[16] *Ibid.*

self-affirmations, the imagination of distinction, relation, balance, and hierarchic order often appears. Nevertheless, Lawrence is essentially like Blake and Nietzsche in his address to the untapped powers of man and his hatred of the rules and forms that curb those powers.

The Utopian Vision of D. H. Lawrence, University of Chicago Press, 1963, pp. 149–59.

GEORGE A. PANICHAS

Voyage of Oblivion

D. H. Lawrence's preoccupation with the meaning of death is nowhere more powerfully and memorably seen than in his volume of poetry published posthumously under the title *Last Poems* ... There can be little doubt that these poems embody Lawrence's most fervent religious expression as well as the final significance of his religious quest and message ...

In the first of Lawrence's death-poems, 'Bavarian Gentians', originally entitled 'Glory of Darkness' and written in Baden-Baden in 1929, not only the quality of reverence but also that of tranquillity becomes quite evident. The poem, with its mythological framework, is one of Lawrence's finest. Entirely free of any kind of intellectualized deliberateness, it arises from the deepest part of the soul, from 'simple, sensuous, passionate life'. In it the poet shows that death is a continuing part of a great mystery, transcending limitations of formal definition and academic explanation ...

In 'Bavarian Gentians' we see the lonely but resolute figure of the religious seeker continuing on his way into 'that sightless realm where darkness is awake upon the dark'.

> Not every man has gentians in his house
> in soft September, at slow, sad Michaelmas,

the poem begins with masterful and majestic restraint. The reference to Michaelmas (the feast day of the archangel Michael) is an interesting one, since along with references to Pluto and Demeter and Persephone, it again shows Lawrence's characteristic synthesis of Christian and pagan symbols. (For Lawrence, of course, religion was not a matter of revolution or of distinction between the old and the new—for instance, paganism vs. Christianity—but rather of a continuation of the old and into the new.) As the poem continues, the religious seeker's impassioned appeal found in the line 'lead me then, lead me the way' becomes symbolic of his journey into the dark and unknown realm of death, represented here by the lower world ('Pluto's gloom') of pagan times, and strikingly reiterated in the words associated with darkness and blueness:

> Bavarian gentians, big and dark, only dark
> darkening the day-time torch-like with the
> smoking blueness of Pluto's gloom,

ribbed and torch-like, with their blaze of
    darkness spread blue
down flattening into points, flattened under
    the sweep of white day
torch-flower of the blue-smoking darkness,
    Pluto's dark blue daze,
black lamps from the halls of Dio, burning
    dark blue,
giving off darkness, blue darkness, as
    Demeter's pale lamps give off light,
lead me then, lead me the way.

Here, as throughout the *Last Poems*, death is represented as some
great 'journey' from 'the entanglements of life', as he puts it in 'So
Let Me Live',

to the adventure of death, in eagerness
turning to death, as I turn to beauty
to the breath, that is, of new beauty
    unfolding in death.

In this respect, therefore, 'Bavarian Gentians' sets the theme of all
his death poetry:

Reach me a gentian, give me a torch!
let me guide myself with the blue,
    forked torch of this flower
down the darker and darker stairs,
where blue is darkened on blueness
even where Persephone goes, just now,
    from the frosted September
to the sightless realm where darkness
    is awake upon the dark
and Persephone herself is but a voice
or a darkness invisible enfolded in
    the deeper dark
of the arms Plutonic, and pierced with
    the passion of dense gloom,
among the splendour of torches of
    darkness, shedding darkness on
the lost bride and her groom.

Death, Lawrence maintains, is not easy—'O it is not easy to die the
death', he writes in his poem 'Difficult Death'. In this poem he
characteristically refers to death as a journey to a 'dark oblivion'. But
there is no feeling of futility or irremediable grief.

So build your ship of death, and let the
    soul drift
to dark oblivion.
Maybe life is still our portion
after the bitter passage to oblivion.

In 'All Souls' Day', the same thought is expressed again. The poem contains a deep sense of tender compassion; the first line pleads with the living to

> Be careful, then, and be gentle about
>   death.
> For it is hard to die, it is difficult
>   to go through
> the door, even when it opens.

The poet then goes on to describe the dead who have departed from 'the walled and silvery city of the now hopeless body', lingering for a time 'in the shadow of the earth':

> For the soul has a long, long journey
>   after death
> to the sweet home of pure oblivion.
> Each needs a little ship, a little ship
> and the proper store of meal for the
>   longest journey.
>
> Oh, from out of your heart
> provide for your dead once more, equip them
> like departing mariners, lovingly.

In the course of these poems Lawrence clearly differentiates between the dead who depart for the new journey with a feeling of quiet contentment and those 'unhappy dead' who in actual life failed to affirm the creative meaning of being. Concerning the latter, he writes with some indignation in the poem 'Death':

> They dare not die, because they know
> in death they cannot any more escape
> the retribution for their obstinacy.
> Old men, old obstinate men and women
> dare not die, because in death
> their hardened souls are washed with
>   fire, and washed and seared
> till they are softened back to life-
>   stuff again, against which they
>   hardened themselves.

Or again, as he writes in 'Two Ways of Living and Dying':

> But when people are only self-conscious
>   and self-willed
> they cannot die, their corpse still runs on,
> while nothing comes from the open heaven,
>   from earth, from the sun and moon
> to them, nothing, nothing.

The latter are unhappy precisely because they have not lived and have denied creative life all along, a denial which to Lawrence is the greatest of evils. . . . This feeling is registered in the poem 'The Houseless Dead', which describes the inability of those who have denied life to continue the mysterious and wondrous journey into the realm of death:

> Oh pity the dead that were ousted out
> of life
> all unequipped to take the long, long
> voyage.
> Gaunt, gaunt they crowd the gray mud-
> beaches of shadow
> that intervene between the final sea
> and the white shores of life.

Such life-deniers, Lawrence continues, are really incapable of dying, for they have always been dead:

> The poor gaunt dead that cannot die
> into the distance with receding oars,
> but must roam like outcast dogs on
> the margins of life!

In another poem, 'Beware the Unhappy Dead!', he draws a close connection between the 'houseless', 'uneasy' dead and death-in-life. The poem starts with a warning:

> Beware the unhappy dead thrust out of life
> unready, unprepared, unwilling, unable
> to continue on the longest journey.

Lawrence then seeks to show that the 'lost souls' and 'angry dead' who crowd 'the long mean marginal stretches of our existence' are in reality those living dead who never really died because they never really lived. As such their presence disturbs the atmosphere and they haunt life with 'disembodied rage' . . . The result, naturally, is the perpetuity of a condition of living death ('Oh, now they moan and throng in anger') in the stagnancy of human existence:

> Oh, but beware, beware the angry dead.
> Who knows, who knows how much our
> modern woe
> is due to the angry unappeased dead
> that were thrust out of life, and now
> come back at us
> malignant, malignant, for we will not
> succour them.

Yet, it is on a confident note that Lawrence often ends. For, as he writes in his essay 'On Human Destiny', 'The exquisite light of ever-renewed human consciousness is never blown out'. And in the lines

that follow directly those quoted above, he shows that the human
condition is surely not beyond hope of change:

> Oh on this day for the dead, now November
>   is here
> set a place for the dead, with a cushion
>   and soft seat
> and put a plate, and put a wine-glass out
> and serve the best food, the fondest wine
> for your dead, your unseen dead, and with
>   your hearts
> speak with them and give them peace and
>   do them honour.

Nevertheless, Lawrence does not attempt to speculate in absolute
terms about the nature of life-after-death, and this accounts for his
repeated use of such words as 'darkness' and 'oblivion' throughout the
death-poems. His approach to death and the after-life can be seen,
for example, in the poem, 'Song of Death', wherein he speaks of the
'utter peace' that is gained in the 'oblivion where the soul at last is
lost'. The mystery of death, like the mystery of life, cannot be ex-
plained away or defined in any absolute terms. For, as he writes in
'The End, the Beginning':

> If there were not an utter and absolute dark
> of silence and sheer oblivion
> at the core of everything,
> how terrible the sun would be,
> how ghastly it would be to strike a match,
> and make a light.

Death, consequently, is not only a kind of 'utter and absolute dark', a
'silence', a 'sheer oblivion', 'a silent sheer cessation of all awareness',
but also a form of sleep in which there is 'a hint of lovely oblivion'
('Sleep'), the 'sleep of God', in which 'the world is created afresh'
('Sleep and Waking') . . .

In the process of death, hence, Lawrence sees the death of the old,
knowing self, and the birth of a new man. In 'Gladness of Death' he
puts it in this way:

> I can feel myself unfolding in the dark
>   sunshine of death
> to something flowery and fulfilled, and with
>   a strange sweet perfume.
> Men prevent one another from being men
> but in the great spaces of death
> the winds of the afterwards kiss us
>   in blossom of manhood.

Lawrence's concept of decay and corruption, followed by rebirth and
renewal, can be seen especially in the beautiful poem 'Shadows', which

begins with a longing for peace in the sleep of death and in 'the hands of God':

> And if tonight my soul may find her peace
> in sleep, and sink in good oblivion,
> and in the morning wake like a new-opened
>   flower
> then I have been dipped again in God, and
>   new-created.

The feelings then recounted are those in which the poet recognizes the ultimate meaning of the experience of death and rebirth:

> And if, as the weeks go round, in the dark of
>   the moon
> my spirit darkens and goes out, and soft
>   strange gloom
> pervades my movements and my thoughts
>   and words
> then I shall know that I am walking still
> with God, we are close together now the
>   moon's in shadow.

The lines that follow are endemic to most of Lawrence's death-poetry, with references to autumn, to 'the pain of falling leaves', to 'dissolution and distress'. Death is not some new experience in remote isolation, but one that is closely associated with Lawrence's 'vital and magnificent God', whose presence is a crucial one in the process of death:

> And if, as autumn deepens and darkens
> I feel the pain of falling leaves, and
>   stems that break in storms
> and trouble and dissolution and distress
> and then the softness of deep shadows
>   folding, folding
> around my soul and spirit, around my lips
> so sweet, like a swoon, or more like the
>   drowse of a low, sad song
> singing darker than the nightingale, on,
>   on to the solstice
> and the silence of short days, the silence
>   of the year, the shadow,
> then I shall know that my life is moving
>   still
> with the dark earth, and drenched
> with the deep oblivion of earth's lapse and
>   renewal.

> And if, in the changing phases of man's life
> I fall in sickness and in misery
> my wrists seem broken and my heart seems dead
> and strength is gone, and my life
> is only the leavings of a life:

and still, among it all, snatches of lovely
   oblivion, and snatches of renewal
odd, wintry flowers upon the withered stem,
   yet new, strange flowers
such as my life has not brought forth before,
   new blossoms of me—
then I must know that still
I am in the hands of the unknown God,
he is breaking me down to his oblivion
to send me forth on a new morning, a new man.

From *Adventure in Consciousness: The Meaning of D. H.
Lawrence's Religious Quest,* by George A. Panichas (The Hague,
1964), Chapter VIII, pp. 180–92.

Select Bibliography

WORKS

FICTION
Complete Editions
   The novels and short stories of D. H. Lawrence are available in the Phoenix (Heinemann) and Penguin editions.

POEMS
The Complete Poems of D. H. Lawrence, Collected and Edited with an Introduction and Notes by Vivian de Sola Pinto and Warren Roberts, 2 vols. London: Heinemann, 1964.

LETTERS
The Letters of D. H. Lawrence, ed. Aldous Huxley. London: Heinemann, 1932, repr. 1956. Contains Huxley's well-known Introduction defending Lawrence as a religious artist.

ESSAYS
Selected Essays, with an Introduction by Richard Aldington. London: Penguin Books, 1968.
Phoenix: The Posthumous Papers of D. H. Lawrence, ed. E. D. MacDonald. London: Heinemann, 1961.
Sex, Literature and Censorship, ed. Harry T. Moore. New York: Compass Books, 1953.
Psychoanalysis and the Unconscious and *Fantasia of the Unconscious* with an Introduction by Philip Rieff. New York: Compass Books, 1960.

LITERARY CRITICISM
Studies in Classic American Literature. London: Collins, 1955.
Selected Literary Criticism, ed. Anthony Beal. London: Heinemann, 1955.

BIOGRAPHY

Edward Nehls, *D. H. Lawrence: A Composite Biography*, 3 vols. Madison: University of Wisconsin Press, 1957–9.
F. J. Hoffman and H. T. Moore (eds.), *The Achievement of D. H. Lawrence*. Norman: University of Oklahoma Press, 1953.
J. Middleton Murry, *Son of Woman: The Story of D. H. Lawrence*. London: Cape, 1931. The most notorious and hostile account of Lawrence's life. For a slightly more balanced account, see also Murry's *Reminiscences of D. H. Lawrence* (London: Cape, 1933).
Jessie Chambers (pseud. E.T.), *D. H. Lawrence: A Personal Record*. London: Cape, 1935. An invaluable account of Lawrence's early development by the girl who inspired the character of Miriam in *Sons and Lovers*.
Frieda Lawrence, *Not I, but the Wind*. London: Heinemann, 1935.
Catherine Carswell, *The Savage Pilgrimage: A Narrative of D. H. Lawrence*. London: Martin Secker, 1932. (Revised Edition, London, Secker

& Warburg, 1951.) An admirable corrective to Middleton Murry's attack on Lawrence in *Son of Woman*.

Richard Aldington, *Portrait of a Genius, but . . ., The Life of D. H. Lawrence, 1885–1930*. London: Heinemann, 1950.

Harry T. Moore, *The Intelligent Heart: The Story of D. H. Lawrence*. London: Heinemann, 1954; Penguin.

CRITICISM

Father William Tiverton (pseud. William Robert Jarrett-Kerr), *D. H. Lawrence and Human Existence*. London: Rockliff, 1951. Preface by T. S. Eliot. An attempt to represent Lawrence as on the whole suitable for Christian readers.

F. R. Leavis, *D. H. Lawrence: Novelist*. London: Chatto & Windus, 1955; Penguin, 1964.

Mark Spilka, *The Love Ethic of D. H. Lawrence*. Bloomington: Indiana University Press, 1955.

Graham Hough, *The Dark Sun: A Study of D. H. Lawrence*. London: Duckworth, 1956.

Eliseo Vivas, *D. H. Lawrence: The Failure and the Triumph of Art*. Evanston: Northwestern University Press, 1960. Rather hostile and impatient criticism, but interesting as an attempt to make Lawrence out to be a new kind of novelist who abandoned the traditional novel-form.

S. L. Goldberg, '*The Rainbow*: Fiddle-Bow and Sand', in *Essays in Criticism*, XI (October 1961). Stresses the 'emotional falsity of the last few pages' of *The Rainbow*, and finds the 'second half of the novel weaker than the first'. Should be read in conjunction with Edward Engelberg's defence of the ending of *The Rainbow* in the article printed in this book.

Eugene Goodheart, *The Utopian Vision of D. H. Lawrence*. Chicago and London: University of Chicago Press, 1963. Places Lawrence within the European tradition including such writers as Kierkegaard, Nietzsche and Dostoevsky. Philosophically interesting, but strays rather far from a critical consideration of Lawrence's actual writing.

George A. Panichas, *Adventure in Consciousness: The Meaning of D. H. Lawrence's Religious Quest*. The Hague: Mouton & Co., 1964.

H. M. Daleski, *The Forked Flame: A Study of D. H. Lawrence*. London: Faber, 1965. A carefully-presented and well-argued account of the 'duality' of Lawrence's view of life as revealed in his fiction and non-fiction.

Keith Sagar, *The Art of D. H. Lawrence*. London: Cambridge University Press 1966. One of the best books on Lawrence of recent years.